YOUNG STUDENTS

Learning Library®

VOLUME 14

Model Making—Netherlands

NEWFIELD
PUBLICATIONS

MIDDLETOWN·CONNECTICUT

Young Students Learning Library is a federally registered trademark of Newfield Publications, Inc.

ISBN 0-8374-0484-3

1993 Edition

CONTENTS

MODEL MAKING Playing with dolls, running a toy car, building a toy town, running an electric train—in all these activities you use models. The toy car, the doll, the buildings, and the train are all models of larger, real objects.

Models are not always smaller. Sometimes they are the same size as the real object (such as a play telephone), and sometimes they are larger (such as a model of a tiny insect). There are two kinds of models. One kind is a copy of something that is already in existence. A model car, airplane, or house, a model of an animal or a skeleton, a model of the atoms that make up a molecule—any of these things are reproductions, or models, of things that already exist. The second type of model is made by designing something that does not exist now or has not existed in the past. A model of a car of the future or a new kind of airplane that has never before existed are examples of this type of model.

Models are used for educational purposes. They give you experiences that you could not otherwise have. By using models, you can see what a city on the moon might look like in the year 2300, or you can discover what an Indian village of long ago was like.

Some people earn their living making models. The models they make may be *architectural*—to show what buildings will look like before they are built. Some models are *industrial*—to be used as test models, such as an airplane in a wind tunnel. Other industrial models are used to show what a product will look like before it is manufactured in great quantities. *Educational* models are used in teaching. A model of the human heart can help students understand more about the human body. A model of a city can help planners and government officials understand its needs and help them plan the city's future.

Models are often constructed during the making of a movie, when it would be very expensive to film the real thing, such as a battleship in a storm at sea.

A professional model maker uses many kinds of materials, but good models can be made with ordinary, inexpensive materials. Cardboard tubes, paper, strong glue, balsa wood, wire, and plasticine clay are good basic materials. You can also buy model-making kits for spaceships, airplanes, automobiles, and ships. These kits provide all the materials and instructions that you will need.

■ LEARN BY DOING

Making a Model Room First, find a cardboard box, such as a shoe box. Remove the lid, and place the box on its side. The inside of the box will be the room. Cut out windows or draw them on the walls. Then paint the walls, ceiling, and floor with tempera paints. You can make furniture using strong glue and various kinds of materials—matchboxes or other small boxes, spools, small plastic or paper cups, caps from spray cans or bottle tops, plasticine clay, or paper sculpture. Scraps of cloth can be used for rugs, curtains, tablecloths, and bedspreads. You may even want to paint some of the furniture.

Making a Model of a Car Imagine a car of the future and how it might look. On a piece of paper, sketch the side, rear, and front views of your car. Using plasticine clay, mold the car into the shape you have drawn. Your model may also be carved from wood or soap, or you may want to use paper sculpture. ■

ALSO READ: CARVING, CLAY MODELING, PAPER SCULPTURE.

▲ *Models in movie-making: Supergirl, filmed in England, employed two model workshops to create special effects.*

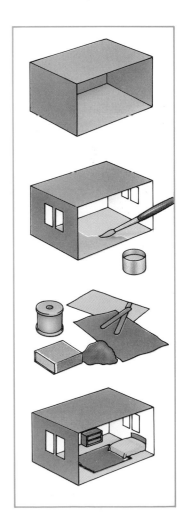

◀ *Harvesting seaweed—a plentiful natural resource—in Japan where people eat seaweeds. The seaweed grows on nets from which it is gathered. (See* NATURAL RESOURCES.*)*

▲ The Women of Avignon, *by Pablo Picasso.*

▶ *Detail from* Cathedral *(1947) painted by the American abstract artist Jackson Pollock, which uses enamel and aluminum paint on canvas. This thicket of lines is very busy to look at. Pollock painted with his canvas on the floor so he could "literally be in the painting" as he explained.*

MODERN ART Every age in history has had its modern artists. They have most often been young people with new ideas different from those their masters were teaching. "Modern art," as we define it today, is a particular kind of art. Modern art is sometimes not *representational*—it doesn't have to look like anything. It may be just a pleasant blend of colors representing nothing more than the way the artist feels. Some contemporary (of our time) artists are *not* modern in their work—artists such as Andrew Wyeth. But very many contemporary artists work in modern art.

Modern art began in the second half of the 1800's, after the camera was invented. Photographs pictured things exactly as they were. So some artists saw no reason to do the same thing. Artists no longer had to paint portraits of children so their families would remember how they looked when they were little. A camera was better than an artist for that.

The French painter, Paul Cézanne, made the first great breakthrough to modern art. He worked slowly and carefully. He studied color and composition. He even destroyed many of his works before finally reaching a

new kind of art. He felt that the shapes in a painting counted most. He thought that all objects were one of three shapes—cylinder, sphere, or cone. A human body is a cylinder, a head a sphere. Three people together can form a cone shape. He changed the shapes of objects he painted, if he thought it would make a better picture. Cézanne used color to show perspective and three dimensions in a picture. His colors were bright, and he let the brush strokes show in his finished pictures. Cézanne was the pathfinder who led other artists to freer thinking in art.

Painting at about the same time as Cézanne was a Dutchman named Vincent van Gogh. He used paints strewn with grains of pigment that gave a lively look to the surface of his pictures. He used bright, new color combinations that showed his strong feelings. Sometimes he got so emotional when painting that he pressed paints right out of the tubes onto the canvas without blending them. Van Gogh was the first of the *expressionists*, modern artists who painted to express feelings.

One of the great modern artists, Paul Gauguin, lived for a while with van Gogh. Gauguin then went to the South Pacific to paint. The beautiful, golden-colored people and the lush, tropical plants suited his kind of art. Gauguin would *abstract*—he would paint only those parts of a scene that he wanted. He simplified scenes to make patterns.

Another painter who loved color was Henri Matisse. His use of bright colors gave him and his followers the name of *Les Fauves*—The Wild Animals. Matisse was the leader of *Les Fauves*. Bright colors, strong lines and patterns, and a kind of joy in painting were his gift to art.

At about the same time as Matisse, another artist was developing in Paris—Pablo Picasso, probably the best-known modern artist. He and Georges Braque developed *cubism*, in which the artist tries to show all the sides of an object. Picasso created the huge canvas, *The Women of Avignon*, shown here. Looking at the picture at first is a bit of a shock. Picasso has sharpened the shapes of the women on the left. The two on the right have faces that are pulled out of shape. Besides the exaggerated features, you can see that the figures are made up of wedges or angular pieces—in the many surfaces of cubism. The whole picture is fitted together tightly. Picasso moved on to other styles, but cubism as a style, remained popular.

After cubism arrived, breaking a painting into three-dimensional-looking chunks, it was only a step to *nonobjective painting*, which does not even try to look like real objects. The leading nonobjective artists were Vassily Kandinsky of Russia and Piet Mondrian of the Netherlands. Kandinsky felt that art should come from the inner self—no model to look at, no landscape to see when painting. His pictures have titles such as *Red Spot* and *Composition Number Four*, which is shown here. Bright color, irregular lines, and surprising curves

▲ Composition Number Four, *by Vassily Kandinsky.*

fill his paintings. Mondrian carefully planned his paintings in a precise, exact way, marking off sections of color in various sizes.

Abstract expressionism became popular in the 1950's. A well-known abstract expressionist was Mark Rothko, whose painting *Composition* is shown here. Abstract expressionism was called "action painting," because the artists put their whole selves into it. Some artists spray or pour the paint on, working with the canvas on the floor. Jackson Pollock, a well-known U. S. artist whose painting *Cathedral* is shown on the facing page, worked in this way.

Pop art became popular in the 1960's. Artists copied advertising art, such as the label of a tomato soup can. New kinds of art keep appearing. Critics constantly disagree on what is "good" modern art. The new trends in painting need the test of years before it becomes clear whether the art is "good" or if it will go out of style and be forgotten.

ALSO READ: ABSTRACT ART; CÉZANNE, PAUL; EXPRESSIONISM; GAUGUIN, PAUL; IMPRESSIONISM; MATISSE, HENRI; PICASSO, PABLO; SURREALISM; VAN GOGH, VINCENT.

▼ Joseph's Liquor (1980), *by Robert Cottingham, shows the artist's fascination with street "furniture," including the "pop" art of commercial advertising.*

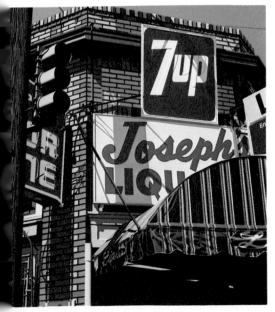

▼ Composition, *by Mark Rothko.*

MODERN DANCE see DANCE.

▲ *Tourists admire the varied and ever-changing patterns of the beautiful sand dunes found in parts of the Mohave Desert.*

In the 1890's, prospectors looking for gold and silver came to the Mohave Desert. Only a few struck it rich. Today, valuable deposits of boron (a mineral used in jet and rocket fuels) and sodium sulfate are found there. Miners also drill for tungsten and other space-age metals.

ALSO READ: CALIFORNIA, DESERT.

MOLD see FUNGUS.

MOLECULE see CHEMISTRY.

MOHAVE DESERT The Mohave, or Mojave, Desert lies in southern California near Los Angeles. Along with the adjoining Colorado Desert, this wasteland covers about 20,000 square miles (50,000 sq. km), four times the size of the state of Connecticut.

The winds that blow eastward off the Pacific lose almost all of their moisture as they pass over the Coastal Range and the Sierra Nevada mountains. They have little moisture left to drop on the Mohave's dry sands. Any moisture is sucked up by intense desert heat. The record-high temperature in the United States was recorded in Death Valley, part of the Mohave, on July 10, 1913. It was 134 degrees Fahrenheit (56.6° C) *in the shade!*

The desert terrain consists of desert basins, low mountain ranges, outcroppings of lava, and cinder cones of extinct volcanoes. A few desert-type plants and animals live there. Cactus plants store water in their thick stems. Grasshopper mice feed on scorpions and other small prey.

Some intermittent streams are present in the valleys of the desert. The largest, the Mohave River, flows mainly underground. In Antelope Valley in the western part, farmers draw up underground water to irrigate crops such as alfalfa. Well water from the Mohave is piped to surrounding resort areas, such as Palm Springs and Palm Desert, and used to wet down golf courses.

Millions of years ago the Mohave Desert was covered by the Pacific Ocean. Then the coastal mountains were pushed up, cutting off the Mohave from the sea.

MOLES AND SHREWS These animals are insectivores, which means "insect eaters." All insectivores look somewhat alike. Most have small, furry bodies and long, pointed noses. Their feet have tough, sharp claws that allow them to dig quickly through the ground. As the word insectivores tells you, they all eat insects, but they may also eat worms and other small, crawling animals. Moles and shrews are useful to farmers and gardeners because they get rid of many pests.

Moles are about 6 inches (15 cm) long. They have thick fur on their

▼ *Moles make complicated underground tunnel systems that include sleeping and nesting chambers. Some chambers are also used for storing food. Excavated soil is pushed up to form molehills.*

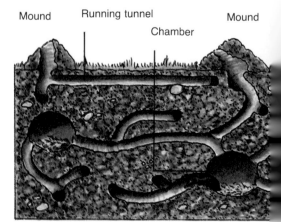

Mound   Running tunnel   Mound
                    Chamber

Common shrew

Hedgehog

▲ *Shrews are fierce little animals. Their sharp teeth make it easy for them to kill and eat their prey. Hedgehogs are covered with sharp pointed quills. Their quills are set close together, making a protective covering against predators.*

bodies, but their pink tails have no fur. A mole's powerful front legs and claws turn outward, enabling it to tunnel rapidly through the earth. A mole can dig as much as 50 yards (45 m, or half the length of a football field!) underground in an hour. Moles dig almost constantly because they are looking for worms and insects to eat. If a mole could not find food for even 10 or 11 hours, it would die of starvation. Moles are almost blind because they spend all of their lives in their underground burrows and tunnels. Moles live in underground nests and tunnel away from the nests in search of food. They get rid of earth dug from their tunnels by pushing it upward. This forms the molehills that we often see in gardens.

A shrew is a furry creature about the size of a small mouse. It looks like a mouse, except for its pointed snout. One kind of shrew, the white-toothed *pygmy shrew*, is the smallest nonflying mammal in the world. It is only about 2 inches (5 cm) long and weighs about as much as a penny.

Shrews are very active animals. A shrew has an enormous appetite, considering its size. A shrew eats three or four times its own weight in insects, worms, and mice every day. The shrew, like the mole, must eat almost constantly to live.

A shrew is a very nervous animal. It will sometimes die of fright if it hears a loud, sudden noise. But the shrew will fight other larger animals. Like the mole, the shrew lives alone. Shrews have a disagreeable odor that prevents many of their enemies from bothering them. Some shrews have a poisonous bite.

Shrews live mostly in gardens and wooden areas. But people rarely see them, because they come out only at night and spend almost all their time hidden under leaves and bushes, eating and eating.

Hedgehogs are larger than most insectivores and live in Europe. They are about 10 inches (25 cm) long. Instead of fur, the hedgehog has tiny quills like the quills of a porcupine. When a hedgehog is attacked by another animal, it rolls itself up into a ball with its quills sticking out everywhere. But if a fox finds a rolled-up hedgehog, the fox will push the hedgehog into water. The hedgehog must then unroll to swim. As it swims, the fox can catch it.

The white-toothed pigmy shrew is not only the smallest mammal in the world. It also has the shortest life span. Most shrews die before they are one year old.

▼ *The mole spends nearly all of its time tunneling through the soil with its huge, spadelike front legs. It eats insects and earthworms.*

1623

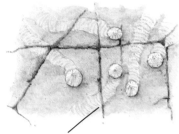

Feeding trail

▲ *Limpets, which are in the gastropod class of mollusks, are found all over the exposed rocks of the shore. When the tide is in, they move around, scraping algae off the rocks with a rasplike mouth part. This leaves a "trail" on the rock.*

▼ *The muscular piddock is strong enough to make holes in soft rocks. Its siphon protrudes from the opening to breathe and feed. The piddock is a bivalve mollusk.*

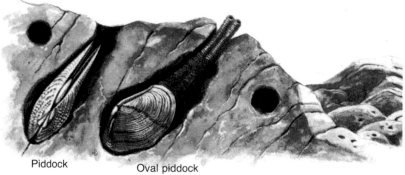

Piddock   Oval piddock

The hedgehog makes its home under hedges and bushes. It comes out at night to feed on beetles, snails, worms, frogs, mice, and even poisonous snakes. The hedgehog has a high level of immunity to snake poison. When winter comes, the hedgehog builds a warm nest of leaves in its underground burrow. Then the hedgehog goes to sleep until spring comes again.

ALSO READ: MAMMAL.

MOLLUSK The most familiar mollusks are probably the popular seafoods, such as clams and oysters. But there are more than 40,000 kinds of mollusks. They vary in size and shape—from tiny sluglike animals that could fit on the head of a pin to the giant squid.

Mollusks live on land, in salt water, and in fresh water throughout the temperate and tropical regions of the world. Certain snails live in the tops of tropical trees. But most mollusks live in the deep oceans.

Common Features of Mollusks
All mollusks are related, or alike, in certain ways. The word "mollusk" comes from a Latin word meaning "soft." Mollusks are *invertebrates*, having no bones at all. Their bodies are soft and somewhat shapeless. They have no joints or outer body parts, as do most other animals.

SHELL. Most mollusks have a hard shell that protects their soft bodies. Most of the shell is made of calcium carbonate. The inner surface of the shell of some mollusks is an iridescent, pearly layer. The shapes of mollusk shells vary greatly, but certain similar characteristics within each group serve as the basis for classification and identification.

Although a hard outer shell is typical of mollusks, some mollusks, such as slugs and squids, have shells inside the body, which are often very small. Octopuses have no shell.

INTERNAL ANATOMY. A mollusk's soft body is surrounded by an enveloping layer of tissue, called a *mantle*. Glands in the mantle produce the substances that harden to form the shell. In some mollusks, the mantle also performs other functions. The mantle of a clam has tube-shaped folds, called siphons, that help the clam eat and breathe.

Mollusks can stretch their bodies in and out of their shells by using strong muscles. The major means of movement is a muscular "foot." The size and shape of the foot is different in each group of mollusks, enabling it to be used for creeping, digging, or swimming.

Marine mollusks breathe through gills. Blood vessels, containing red, yellow, and colorless blood, carry oxygen-filled blood to the heart. Land mollusks also have gills, but they serve no purpose. Land mollusks breathe through pulmonary sacs formed from the mantle, which are similar to the sacs in lungs.

Most mollusks have a mouth, short gullet, fairly large stomach, and a long intestine. Inside the mouth is the *radula*, an organ like a file, which is used for scraping food off rocks or boring through hard substances. (A mollusk might bore a hole into sand or through the shell of another mollusk.) The stomach is connected to a digestive gland, in which food is absorbed into the blood. The mollusk's nervous system consists of nerve cords connected to masses of nerve cells, called *ganglia*. No ganglion is

▲ *Squids, another kind of mollusk, swim in the sea and feed on prawns and shrimps, which they seize in their tentacles.*

▲ *The shell of bivalve mollusks (top) has two halves, or* valves, *hinged at the top. Univalves (bottom), have a single, usually coiled valve.*

large enough to be called a "brain."

REPRODUCTION. All mollusks hatch from eggs. In some mollusks, the eggs are fertilized while still inside the mother's body. Then they are laid in the sand under the water until they are ready to hatch. But in most mollusks, the eggs are released and then covered by sperm. Most of the eggs hatch as larvae, or immature animals very unlike their parents in appearance. Other mollusks, such as octopuses, look like tiny adults when they hatch.

How Mollusks Are Classified Mollusks are divided into six classes. The most primitive class, *Monoplacophora*, contains the "living fossil" *Neopilina*, which looks a bit like a limpet. The class *Amphineura* includes the chitons, whose shells consist of eight overlapping plates. Members of the class *Scaphopoda* have open-ended shells resembling an elephant's tusks. The tusk shell, or tooth shell, uses its small pointed foot to dig in sand. All these mollusks live in the sea, either at great depth or along the seashore.

GASTROPODS. Snails, abalones, and conchs belong to the class called *Gastropoda*. These are *univalve* (one-shelled) mollusks, with spiral-shaped shells. At the end of a gastropod's foot is a hard "door." When the foot is drawn into the body, the door fits snugly into the shell's opening. Many gastropods are able to seal themselves inside their shells. Some gastropods attach themselves to rocks. The abalone can fasten itself to a rock so tightly that only a knife can pry it loose.

PELECYPODS. Mollusks of the class *Pelecypoda* are "bivalves." Their shells have two parts that open and close like a book. Each shell section is called a *valve*. The valves are joined by a muscle that acts like a hinge. The muscle pulls the two valves shut when the animal wants protection. When the valves are open, the soft mantle can be seen. Sometimes it is brightly colored and has a fringe of fingerlike parts.

Bivalve mollusks include clams, oysters, scallops, and mussels. Bivalve mollusks do not have heads. They use their wedge-shaped feet to move around and dig into mud.

CEPHALOPODS. Octopuses, squids, cuttlefish, and nautiluses belong to the class *Cephalopoda*. These mollusks have reached a high state of development. Like other mollusks, they have soft bodies and mantles. But they do not look like other mollusks, and they have very different habits. The shells of squids, octopuses, and cuttlefish are inside their bodies. These mollusks have numerous arms, or tentacles, which help them move or hold their prey. Octopuses, squids, and cuttlefish are able to protect themselves by shooting an inky fluid into the water to hide themselves. The *chambered nautilus* has an outer shell that is divided into chambers. As a new chamber grows, the nautilus moves into it, closes off the old one, and carries the entire shell along as it moves.

Giant squids are the largest mollusks, sometimes growing to 55 feet

Giant squid probably spend most of their lives in deep water, but sometimes they may venture near the surface. Brief sightings of these huge sea animals may have started some of the legends about sea serpents and other monsters. According to Norse legend, a *kraken* was supposed to be about a mile long. It was said to snatch crewmen from ships with its long tentacles.

▲ *A pearl oyster opened to reveal the pearls inside. The oyster builds pearls by coating small foreign bodies, such as particles of sand, with layers of a substance called* nacre.

Mollusks are little more than efficient sieves. They continually draw in a large amount of water and pump it over their gills to get food and oxygen. The Pacific oyster can take in as much as six gallons (24 liters) of water an hour.

(17 m) long. They are swift swimmers, propelling themselves by ejecting streams of water, just as a jet plane is propelled by the streams of hot gas from its engines.

Valuable and Destructive Mollusks
Many kinds of bivalve mollusks are popular as seafood—especially oysters, clams, and scallops. But at least one bivalve is a destructive enemy of people. Shipworms are small bivalves that grow sharp-edged shells. They use these shells to tunnel through wood beneath the water, such as ship hulls and dock pilings, where they remain for the rest of their lives. As the body of the shipworm grows, the shell bores deeper into the wood, often causing dangerous and costly damage.

Some bivalves, such as the pearl oyster and freshwater mussel, occasionally produce pearls used as jewels. Some bivalve shells are also sources of mother-of-pearl. Mollusk shells that have unusual or beautiful shapes are used as ornaments.

In some countries, octopuses and snails are considered to be great delicacies to eat. Snails are often kept in aquariums to eat any waste and to keep water clean. But some land snails and slugs are common garden and greenhouse pests.

ALSO READ: ANIMAL KINGDOM, CLAMS AND OYSTERS, EGG, HOBBY, MARINE LIFE, OCTOPUS, PEARL, SHELL, SNAILS AND SLUGS, ZOOLOGY.

MOLTING Insects, crustaceans, and certain other invertebrate animals, as well as reptiles, amphibians, birds, and many mammals, go through a process called molting. They shed their hair, feathers, shell, or skin. When one covering is shed, a new one is grown. Molting is controlled by *hormones*, the chemical messengers of the body. *Ecdysone* is the molting hormone of insects.

Insect larvae have a hard outer skin, called a *cuticle*. The cuticle cannot grow or stretch. As the larva grows, it must shed its old cuticle and grow a new one that will fit. Insect larvae may molt as many as 20 times while they are developing. Molting is part of the insect development called *metamorphosis*.

The hard covering of a crustacean, such as a crab, is called a *shell*. When crustaceans molt, the new shell underneath the discarded shell is soft. Before the new shell hardens, the crustacean takes quantities of water into its body to make it swell. The soft shell expands and hardens over an extra-large body. When the water is released the crustacean's body becomes smaller and there is room in the shell to grow.

Snakes, lizards, and amphibians molt by shedding their dead outer skin. The coloring of the skin becomes dull a few days before molting, and the covering of the eye turns cloudy. The animal stretches its skin by swelling some veins near the surface of its head. The skin splits, and the animal crawls out. You can some-

▼ *A timber rattlesnake sheds its skin, which remains clinging to a branch after the snake has crawled out of it.*

times find the skins left by snakes that have molted. Amphibians usually swallow the skin they have shed.

The word "molting" is also used to describe the shedding of feathers and hair by birds and mammals. This usually happens twice a year—in spring and in fall. Birds drop off their old feathers and grow new ones. Sometimes this changes the color of the feathers, which is important in mating and for hiding from enemies. Mammals shed hair in the spring. This makes their coat lighter during summer. In winter, they grow a thicker coat.

ALSO READ: AMPHIBIAN, BIRD, CRUSTACEAN, FEATHER, FUR, HAIR, HORMONE, INSECT, LIZARD, MAMMAL, METAMORPHOSIS, REPTILE, SHELL, SKIN, SNAKE.

MONACO The principality of Monaco lies on the French coast called the Riviera. It is squeezed between steep mountains and the Mediterranean Sea. Monaco is called a principality because it is ruled by a prince. The tiny country has an area of less than one square mile (2.5 sq. km). (See the map with the article on EUROPE.)

The capital is Monaco-Ville (Monaco-City). It is built on top of a cliff overlooking the sea. In the old fortresslike palace of Monaco-Ville lives Prince Rainier III. His beautiful wife, Princess Grace, who died in 1982, was the American motion picture star Grace Kelly before her marriage. Palace guards stand watch in candy-striped guardhouses, and the whole city has a charming medieval look. Even so, there are many large modern buildings.

Below the city lies the port of La Condamine. Its small harbor is usually crowded with luxurious yachts. Near the port is the world-famous Oceanographic Museum, with exhibits produced by research and exploration in the oceans and seas of the world. The well-known undersea explorer, Jacques-Yves Cousteau, became director of the museum in 1956. The town of Monte Carlo is also perched high on top of the cliffs across the harbor from Monaco-Ville. Monte Carlo is a resort area with a famous gambling casino, many hotels and lovely flower gardens. It has a reputation as a meeting place for the rich and famous from all over the world.

Monaco's factories produce beer, candy, chemicals, and tobacco. Postage stamps are also an important source of income. But the main industry is tourism. Thousands of visitors arrive every month to enjoy Monaco's beaches and scenery. Many visitors come just for the famous auto races. Drivers from all over the world compete each year in the race known as the Monaco Grand Prix. The race course is only 2 miles (3.2 km) long,

The biggest clam ever caught is in the American Museum of Natural History, in New York City. It weighs 580 pounds (263 kg) and measures 45 inches (1.1 m) across. This giant mollusk was taken from the Great Barrier Reef off the coast of Australia.

With a population of 28,000 in its area of .73 square mile, Monaco has a greater population density than any other country in the world (more than 38,000 per square mile or 14,700 per square km).

MONACO

Capital City: Monaco-Ville (1,800 people).
Area: 0.73 square mile (1.9 sq. km).
Population: 30,000.
Government: Principality.
Natural Resources: None.
Export Products: Most income comes from tourism and gambling.
Unit of Money: French franc.
Official Language: French.

▲ *A portrait in stained glass of St. Benedict, founder of a monastic order in the* A.D. *500's.*

▼ *A monk of the monastery of St. Catherine, located in the Sinai Peninsula in the Middle East. The old Bible he is displaying was hand-copied by monks living long ago. These religious scholars helped keep learning alive in the Middle Ages.*

but the drivers in the race must circle it 100 times through narrow, winding streets.

More than half of the people of Monaco are French. A small number of people are Monégasque and speak a local dialect—a mixture of French and Italian—also called Monégasque. Many wealthy people from France, Italy, the United States, Britain, and other countries live there, mainly because of Monaco's low taxes.

Monaco has been ruled by the Grimaldi family since the 1200's. Prince Rainier III is the thirty-second Grimaldi to rule.

ALSO READ: MEDITERRANEAN SEA.

MONASTIC LIFE A monastery is a building, or a group of buildings, where religious men called *monks* live and work. The word "monastery" comes from a Greek word meaning "living alone." Monks long ago in the early days of the Christian church used to live alone—often going off into the desert to think about God. Most monks have lived in groups since Saint Benedict's rule in the A.D. 500's made monks a kind of family. The chosen leader was called the "abbot" from the Hebrew word *abba*, meaning father, and the monks called each other "brother." Most Christian monks are Roman Catholic. Monasticism also exists in Buddhism and Hinduism. A group of women followed Benedict's rule under the leadership of his twin sister, Saint Scholastica. Such a community came to be called a *convent* and the women *nuns* or *sisters*. Now there are hundreds of orders of nuns in convents throughout the world.

A Christian monastery sometimes has a *cloister*, or covered walkway surrounding an open court (*garth*). There is also a kitchen, a dining hall called a refectory, and a calefactory, or sitting room. The monks grow their own food in the monastery gar-

▲ *The abbey of Monte Cassino, founded by St. Benedict in* A.D. *529, stands on an impressive hill south of Rome, Italy.*

den. There may be a guest house and small buildings for crafts. Many monastic orders have schools, colleges, or universities on the grounds. For many centuries, monks have been devoted teachers and scholars.

Monks have always helped their neighbors. They have taught farming, reading and writing, bread making, wine making, and other skills. Monasteries have traditionally taken in the lame and the sick and have given shelter to travelers.

Everyday monastic life is very busy. Much time is spent in prayer, studying, reading the Scriptures, and working at various tasks. Time is set aside for *contemplation*, or silent thought. Some orders of monks observe a vow of silence. In recent years, many communities of monks have relaxed their rules and given up the observance of silence to make their lives more relevant to life today, and to be of more service to people. Some monks and nuns no longer live in monasteries or convents and mix more freely with people outside their religious community.

The first monastery was built

around A.D. 300 on an island in the Nile River in Egypt by a monk named Pachomius. Saint Augustine, Saint Benedict, and Saint Francis of Assisi founded monastic orders. Today, thousands of men live by the rules laid down by these men, having taken vows (holy promises) of poverty, chastity, and obedience.

Some of the earliest monasteries in North America were founded in what is now California by the Spanish Franciscan friar, Junipero Serra, in the 1700's. Twelve missions were built a day's journey apart. The monks who lived in them helped to spread Christianity among the Indians and worked also to educate the people. The first monastery built in the United States was St. Vincent's Archabbey, founded by German Benedictine monks at Latrobe, Pennsylvania in 1846. One of the best known is Gethsemane near Bardstown, Kentucky. Gethsemane is a Trappist monastery where author and poet, Thomas Merton (1915–1968), was a monk.

ALSO READ: RELIGION, ROMAN CATHOLIC CHURCH.

MONET, CLAUDE (1840–1926)
The French artist, Claude Monet, was born in Paris but grew up in Le Havre. He studied with the landscape painter, Louis Boudin, who encouraged him to paint outdoor scenes in the open air. Monet went on to the School of Fine Arts in Paris, but he did not like the conventional style of painting taught there. He went back to his old teacher and continued to study. At the time, most painters "jotted down" sketchlike paintings of outdoor scenes and then recreated them in larger, more lifelike finished forms in the studio. Monet broke with tradition by making his spontaneous impressions into the finished work.

Painting landscapes outdoors in natural, changing light became the most important subject for Monet. It remained so for the rest of his long life as a painter. He became the leader of a group of painters in Paris who became known as *Impressionists*.

In 1876, he did a series of paintings of scenes in a Paris railway station. The crowds, the steaming engines, the glass roof, and the bril-

Claude Monet liked painting the same subject again and again. He painted Rouen Cathedral 20 times, in different kinds of weather and at different times of day.

◄ The Houses of Parliament, Sunset, *by Claude Monet. National Gallery of Art, Washington, D.C., Chester Dale collection.*

▲ *An ancient coin minted in Syracuse, Greece, in 412 B.C. to commemorate a victory over Athens.*

▼ *Various kinds of rings have been used as money since the days of the ancient Egyptians. In Ireland, the different sizes of these gold rings had different values.*

▶ *Electrum, a rare alloy of gold and silver, was pressed into coins in ancient Asia Minor. The actual size of the coin and an even smaller silver coin are shown on the right.*

liant sky provided Monet with dramatic color contrasts. He was always most interested in the effects of outdoor light and atmosphere. Sometimes he would paint several pictures showing the same subject in different kinds of light. Once he created 15 paintings of the same haystack—painted at different times of the day.

Monet had a hard time making his living as an artist. He was over 40 years old before he was able to buy a house and some land, in Giverny, near Vernon. There he built a Japanese garden and a lily pond. Water lilies became one of his favorite subjects.

■ LEARN BY DOING

Monet felt that shapes were much less important in a painting than color. He enjoyed painting misty scenes in which forms were hard to see. Look at his *Houses of Parliament*, shown on the previous page. The fog rises from the Thames River, and it is hard to make out the exact shapes of the buildings. But the mist creates a mysterious, otherworld mood. Turn to the article on BIG BEN in volume 3 to see a photograph of part of the real British Parliament buildings. Do you get different feelings from the painting and the photograph? If so, think about why this might be. ■

ALSO READ: IMPRESSIONISM.

MONEY Suppose you bought some candy for 20 cents and gave the shopkeeper a dollar. Think how surprised you would be if, instead of 80 cents in change, he or she gave you 10 shells, 15 beads, 2 small animal skins, and a shark's tooth! All these things have at some time been used as money. Money is based on the idea of *value*. People place a value on things that they want and on things that are rare or hard to get. Diamonds, for example, are scarce and have a high value because many people want them. If no one wanted diamonds, they would be worth very little. On the other hand, people do not place a high value on sand. It is easy to get, and a ton of it can be bought for only a few dollars.

Barter Before money was developed, people used to trade by *bartering*. In bartering, people exchanged goods. A pottery maker who wanted a yard (a meter) of woolen cloth might pay for it by giving the weaver two storage jars. The weaver might pay his or her assistant one jar for two days' work.

Mediums of Exchange In some places, certain goods—furs, shells, metals, oxen, and others—became the *medium of exchange*. All goods were given a value that was related to the medium of exchange. A plow might be worth 20 beaver furs, a

horse might be worth 50 furs, and a piece of land might be worth 300 furs. Mediums of exchange were the earliest kind of money, and they all had three characteristics in common. For one reason or another, people wanted them. They could be used over and over again for a fairly long period of time and they were easy to identify. Grain does not make good money because it gets eaten or spoils.

Metals, such as gold, silver, copper, bronze, nickel, and iron were also used as mediums of exchange, but not in the form of coins. The metals were in powder form or made up into *ingots*, or bars, that had to be weighed each time something was bought or sold. Eventually, metals became the main medium of exchange.

Coin Money The earliest known coins were made in Lydia, a little country in what is now Turkey. King Croesus, the ruler, had the coins made of electrum (a mixture of gold and silver). Coins were easier to use than ingots because they could be counted instead of weighed. Each coin had a certain size and was given a certain value depending on the amount of the metal it contained. When money is given a value that is equal to the value of the material it is made of it is called *commodity money*. Commodity money is no longer used in the United States.

Because coins were not weighed, people sometimes cheated by cutting some of the metal off the edges. This lowered the coins' value. To prevent this, little grooves were placed on the edges of high-value coins. A trimmed coin could then be identified by its lack of grooves. You can see these grooves on U. S. dimes, quarters, and half-dollars.

Paper Money Most of the money used today is paper money. Paper money is even handier than coins. A 20 dollar bill is easier to carry around

and keep track of than 80 quarters. Also, people do not try to trim paper money, because the paper trimmings are not worth anything.

Paper money is not commodity money because the paper itself is not worth the amount printed on it. Paper money began as *credit money*. Credit money represents a certain amount of gold or other medium of exchange. If U.S. dollars were credit money, you could exchange a five dollar bill at a bank and get five dollars worth of gold.

U.S. currency used to be credit money, but nowadays it cannot be exchanged for gold. U.S. currency, like that of many other countries, is *fiat money*. Fiat money cannot be exchanged for gold. Its value is determined by the government. The government simply states that this money is the only type that can be used as *legal tender*. Legal tender is the official money of a country and must be used for making payments and settling debts. It must be accepted by those to whom it is offered.

Checks and Credit Cards Today, many people use checks and credit cards in place of cash. When someone writes a check payable to you, he or she is giving you a certain amount of money deposited in a bank. You can take the check to a bank and receive

▲ *A rolling room in the Royal Mint in London, England, in the late 1800's. Whereas a medieval mint was a coin-making workshop, this mint had become a coin-making factory.*

Ancient coins were either cast in molds or hammered out with a hand-held die. Today, minting machines can stamp out as many as 550 coins a minute.

▼ *Paper money was used in the 1800's for fractions of the dollar.*

What's on a note?

Paper money often carries a portrait of a national hero or the head of state. A one dollar bill bears the head of George Washington.

The central bank that issued the bill.

The number of this bill appears on both halves of the bill. If a bill is torn in half, matching sides must be presented for payment.

Printing plate identification number. Some countries include the printer's name.

Seal and letter that identifies the Federal Reserve district where the note was issued.

Signature of the Treasurer of the United States.

The value of the bill is shown in words and figures.

The seal of the United States Treasury in Washington.

Signature of the Secretary of the Treasury.

The year in which the bill was designed.

The largest paper note ever issued was a Chinese one kwang bill. It was in use between 1368 and 1399 during the Ming Dynasty and was 13 × 9 inches (23 × 33 cm).

---

cash. When you buy something with a credit card, you are making a promise to pay later when the bill is sent to you.

United States Money When settlers came to America from Europe, they brought copper, silver, and gold coins from their home countries. Coins of many countries were used in the colonies. Some of these were "pieces of eight"—the name for Spanish dollars of that time. One piece of eight was worth eight smaller coins, called *reals* or *bits*. Some people still say "two bits" to mean a quarter.

The first coins actually made in America were threepence (three-penny), sixpence, and twelvepence pieces, issued in 1652 in the Massachusetts Bay colony. During the American Revolution, the Continental Congress issued paper money. Because this currency could not be exchanged for gold or silver, people stopped using it, and it soon became worthless.

The Constitution of the United States gave Congress the right to coin money and control its value. On April 2, 1792, Congress established the United States Mint. The mint began to make copper, silver, and gold coins in Philadelphia, Pennsylvania. These coins included copper cents and half-cents, silver dimes, half-dimes, quarters, half-dollars, dollars, two-and-one-half dollar gold quarter-eagles, five dollar gold half-eagles, and ten-dollar gold eagles. Later, the mint made two-cent, three-cent, and twenty-cent coins. Nickels were made in 1866 to replace the half-dime. Today's U.S. coins, like the paper money, are fiat money. The metal in a coin is not worth the amount on the coin. In the late 1960's the Federal Government stopped making silver quarters and dimes to save silver. The metal was changed to a layer of copper sandwiched between two layers of nickel. If you look at the edge of a quarter or dime, you can see the layer of copper.

The first denominations of paper money printed by the United States Government were 5, 10, and 20 dollar bills made in 1861. The backs of the bills were printed in green and people called them "greenbacks." Paper money in a greater variety of values was issued by Congress in 1862. The values ranged from one dollar to ten thousand dollars. Since 1969, bills for five hundred, one thousand, five thousand, and ten thousand dollars have no longer been issued.

Private banks in the United States

and elsewhere used to issue their own notes, which could be *redeemed* (cashed in) for gold or silver, but they have given up doing this.

ALSO READ: BANKS AND BANKING, COIN COLLECTING, ECONOMICS, INTERNATIONAL TRADE.

MONGOLIA

MONGOLIA The "Land of the Blue Skies" is one of the least-known countries in the world. Mongolia lies between the former Soviet Union and China in east central Asia. It is officially called the Mongolian People's Republic and unofficially Outer Mongolia. A region to the south, called Inner Mongolia, is part of China. (See the map with the article on ASIA.) Over 700 years ago, Mongolia was the center of the great empire of the Mongol leader, Genghis Khan.

Mongolia is a vast country, more than twice the size of Texas. But much of the land is barren and desolate. The flat, rocky wastes of the Gobi Desert cover a large area of southeastern Mongolia. A few of the rare Przewalski's horses, the oldest living type of wild horse, are found in the desert. Farther north is a region of grassy plains, or *steppes*. The land rises in the west to forested hills and the rugged Altai Mountains. This area is rich in wildlife, with animals such as ermine, sable, otters, moose, and musk deer. Mongolia has many extremes in climate. In the north, the

temperature in winter can fall to 50° F below zero (−45° C). In the south, it can rise to 107° F (42° C) in the summer. Rainfall is very light.

Some Mongols still follow a *nomadic*, or wandering, life. They herd sheep, camels, horses, and yaks, a kind of large ox. Dogs guard the nomads' caravans. The animals in the herds provide the Mongols with milk and meat for food, hair for tent covering, and hides for leather articles. The herders and their families live in *yurts*, or round felt tents on wooden frames. The yurts are folded and packed on the backs of camels as the herders move from place to place in search of grass and water. Children learn at an early age to ride the tough, fast Mongol ponies. Mongols meet for

▲ *Mongolian herdsmen lay the foundations for a circular tent, or* yurt.

MONGOLIA

Capital City: Ulan Bator (510,000 people).
Area: 604,250 square miles (1,565,000 sq. km).
Population: 2,126,000.
Government: Communist republic.
Natural Resources: Coal, copper, phosphates, zinc, molybdenum, tin, tungsten, nickel, fluospar, gold.
Export Products: Livestock, animal products, wool, hides, fluospar, minerals.
Unit of Money: Tughrik.
Official Language: Mongolian.

horse races and archery and wrestling contests each year in Ulan Bator, the capital.

Many Mongols now live on state farms, or cooperatives, controlled by the government. They herd livestock or grow grain. Fur trapping is an important industry in the mountains, and coal is mined for industrial purposes. Textiles, leather, meat, and grain are processed in factories. The religion of most Mongols is Lamaism, or Tibetan Buddhism. In Ulan Bator is an ancient monastery where about ten thousand Buddhist monks once lived.

In the 1300's, Mongolia began to lose the great power it had enjoyed during the time of Genghis Khan and his descendents. Kublai Khan, a grandson of Genghis, had conquered China and ruled lands stretching from the Pacific Ocean to the Black Sea in Europe. The Manchus, an east Asian people who later conquered China in the 1600's, extended their rule over Outer Mongolia. In 1921, with the help of the Soviet Union, Outer Mongolia established itself as an independent state. The Mongolian People's Republic is ruled by a Communist government.

ALSO READ: CHINA; GENGHIS KHAN; PEKING; POLO, MARCO.

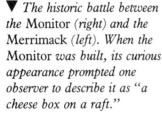

▼ *The historic battle between the* Monitor *(right) and the* Merrimack *(left). When the* Monitor *was built, its curious appearance prompted one observer to describe it as "a cheese box on a raft."*

MONITOR AND MERRIMACK

The famous battle between the *Monitor* and the *Merrimack* in 1862 was the first encounter in history between ironclad warships. This battle was the beginning of the end of wooden warships. It was also one of the first sea battles between ships powered by steam.

During the Civil War, the Confederates wanted to break the Union naval blockade along their seacoast. In the spring of 1862, they raised the frigate, *Merrimack*, which had been sunk. They rebuilt it into an ironclad vessel. They covered the ship's sides with sloping, 4-inch (10-cm) iron plates and placed a strong iron ram on its bow. The ship's name was officially changed to *Virginia*, but people still called it the *Merrimack*.

The strange looking warship sailed into Hampton Roads, Virginia, on March 8, 1862, to shell the wooden ships of the Union fleet anchored there. These ships could not damage the ironclad sides of the *Merrimack*. Their shots bounced off like harmless pebbles. Before leaving because of low tide, the *Merrimack* destroyed two Union ships. The captain planned to return the next day. His idea was to bombard the rest of the Northern fleet and sail up the

Potomac River to shell the capital city, Washington.

However, when the captain sailed into Hampton Roads the next day, he was faced with a warship even stranger looking than the *Merrimack*. It was the *Monitor*, another ironclad ship.

The *Monitor* was designed for the Union navy by a Swedish engineer, John Ericsson. It was constructed partly of iron and partly of wood. Its sides were covered with iron 5 inches (13 cm) thick. A gun turret rose from its deck, which was flat and raftlike, almost level with the water. The turret could turn completely around in a circle and was armed with 11-inch (28-cm) guns.

The two ships faced each other in combat for almost four hours. They shelled each other time after time, but neither could do much damage to the other. The battle was inconclusive, though both sides claimed victory when it finally ended.

Neither ship lasted long after the historic battle. In May 1862, the Confederates blew up the *Merrimack* when they abandoned Norfolk. In December 1862, the *Monitor* sank in rough seas during a violent storm off Cape Hatteras, North Carolina.

But the battle between the *Monitor* and the *Merrimack* was an encounter that changed naval warfare.

ALSO READ: CIVIL WAR, NAVY.

MONKEY Monkeys, apes, and human beings are all primates. They may all be descended from the same ancestor—a tiny, furry animal that lived millions of years ago.

Today, monkeys are classified into two main groups. *New World* monkeys live in the jungles of South America, Mexico, and Central America. *Old World* monkeys live in the jungles of Africa, India, and southeast Asia. Nearly all monkeys eat insects, leaves, and fruit, although some species eat only leaves. Some species eat meat. Most monkeys live in trees, but a few species live on the ground. Monkeys usually live in pairs (male and female) or in groups. Some species are only a few inches in height; others are several feet tall. All monkeys are very good parents.

Some New World monkeys have *prehensile* (grasping) tails. That is, they can use their tails as extra hands—to hang onto branches or to hold things with. Old World monkeys cannot use their tails in this way. In fact, some Old World monkeys do not even have tails. A New World monkey's face looks flat. Its cheeks and nose look as if they have been pushed in. The noses of Old World monkeys stick out more. Old World monkeys can also stretch their cheeks, as you do when you fill your mouth with food or air. They often use those stretchable cheeks for storing food. Old World monkeys have

The Barbary apes on Gibralter are not really apes but monkeys of the macaque family. They were once supposed to have warned the British by barking when the Spanish made a surprise attack. It is believed that Britain will never lose Gibralter as long as the apes remain there.

The noisiest of all monkeys is the howling monkey of South America. In the males, a bone at the top of the windpipe has developed to form a resonant sound-box. The howls, which keep other monkeys away, can be heard for miles.

▲ *A mother baboon protectively cradles her infant. Baboons live in family groups with a complicated social system.*

money. Capuchin monkeys live in the jungle and travel in large groups, chattering and talking among themselves. People in the jungle do not like them. The capuchins are always stealing chickens from the people and eating fruit and vegetables from their gardens.

Spider monkeys have long, thin bodies and very long, strong tails. They use their tails to hold onto things more than any other kind of monkey does. The spider monkey received its name because it can hang from a branch by its tail, like a spider at the end of its thread. Spider monkeys can also grab food with their tails when the food is too far away to get with their hands. They are the best climbers in the jungle, although they do not have thumbs.

Marmosets are a family of small monkeys with fine, soft fur covering their bodies. An adult marmoset is about the size of a squirrel. But the pygmy marmoset grows to only 6 inches (15 cm). Most of them live along the Amazon River in South America. Unlike other New World monkeys, marmosets have only 32 teeth, and they cannot use their tails as extra hands. They have claws on the ends of their fingers and toes instead of fingernails and toenails.

32 teeth, the same number that human beings have. Most New World monkeys have 36 teeth. Old World monkeys also have thick pads, or calluses, growing on their buttocks. The calluses are often brightly colored. New World monkeys do not have these calluses.

Some New World Monkeys *Howling monkeys* can scream very loudly. They can be heard for miles. Sometimes these monkeys will howl together at sunrise or sunset. Howlers are some of the largest monkeys—several feet long. But their brains are small and poorly developed.

Capuchin monkeys are the cleverest of the New World monkeys. They are also called "organ grinder" monkeys because street musicians with hand organs once trained them to collect

Some Old World Monkeys *Macaques* are found everywhere in Africa, India, and Southeast Asia, and also in some areas of the New World. One kind of macaque, called the

▼ *The Barbary ape is the only monkey living in Europe.*

▲ *The spider monkey's tail is prehensile—it is effectively a "fifth hand," used for grasping.*

Barbary ape, lives on the Rock of Gibraltar in southern Europe. The kind of macaque found in India is called the rhesus monkey. This monkey is sacred in the Hindu religion. Scientists often use the rhesus monkey in medical experiments.

Macaques, like other Old World monkeys, live in large groups called *troops*. Each troop has an old male macaque as a leader. The leader always goes ahead of the troop. He looks out for danger and searches for things to eat. If the leader finds an orchard, a cornfield, or a vegetable garden, all the macaques eat as much as they can. If the leader sees anyone coming, he gives a warning cry. The members of the troop then fill their cheeks with extra food and run for the nearest group of trees. The macaques do a great amount of damage to crops.

Baboons and *mandrills* are the largest and fiercest of all the monkeys. They are about the size of a large dog. Like dogs, they have long snouts with very strong jaws and big teeth. Mandrills have colored stripes on their faces that become brighter when the animals are excited. Baboons and mandrills live on the ground in large troops. There might be as many as 100 members in one troop. A troop of baboons is led by the old males. The males stand guard at night and watch out for danger. They also lead the troop on expeditions for food. If a leopard, a lion, or a tiger tries to attack a member of the troop, all the males will attack the animal together. The males may even kill the animal. Baboons and mandrills are not afraid of animals, including human beings.

ALSO READ: APE, CLAWS AND NAILS, HANDS AND FEET, LEMUR, MAMMAL.

MONORAIL see RAILROAD, TRANSPORTATION.

MONROE, JAMES (1758–1831) The fifth President of the United States is best remembered for a statement he made in his annual message to Congress in December 1823. Several Spanish colonies in South America had recently declared their independence. President Monroe announced that any attempt by European powers to set up new colonies in any part of the Americas would be considered an unfriendly act by the United States. This warning, part of the statement known as the *Monroe Doctrine*, became an important part of American foreign policy.

Monroe was born on a small plantation in eastern Virginia. He became a student at the College of William and Mary but left at the age of 17 to fight in the American Revolution. The following year, he was commissioned a lieutenant by General George Washington. Monroe was wounded at the Battle of Trenton, but he recovered and rose to the rank of lieutenant colonel. He served in both the Continental Army and the Virginia militia. During the war, he met Thomas Jefferson, under whom he later studied law. Although not a brilliant student, young Monroe was hardworking and sincere. "He is a man whose soul might be turned wrong side

▲ *The squirrel monkey of the South American rain forests feeds on insects as well as flowers, nuts, and fruit.*

The West African mandrill is the largest of the monkeys. Big males have been reported to weigh well over 100 pounds (45 kg), with a head and body length of more than 3 feet (1 m).

JAMES MONROE
FIFTH PRESIDENT   MARCH 4, 1817–MARCH 4, 1825

Born: April 18, 1758, Westmoreland County, Virginia
Parents: Spence and Elizabeth Jones Monroe
Education: College of William and Mary, Williamsburg, Virginia
Religion: Episcopalian
Occupation: Lawyer
Political Party: Democratic-Republican
State Represented: Virginia
Married: 1786 to Elizabeth Kortright (1768–1830)
Children: Two daughters
Died: July 4, 1831, New York City
Buried: Hollywood Cemetery, Richmond, Virginia

When James Monroe was President, the population of the United States was just over 11 million people.

outwards," said Jefferson, "without discovering a blemish to the world."

The qualities of honesty and courage that had won Thomas Jefferson's admiration made James Monroe popular with the voters of Virginia, and they elected him to several important public offices. He served as a United States senator and twice as governor of Virginia. In 1786, he married Elizabeth Kortright, a beautiful young lady from a fine New York family.

President George Washington appointed Monroe United States minister to France in 1794. Nine years later, after Jefferson became President, Monroe was again sent to France. He helped another United States minister, Robert R. Livingston, to arrange for the purchase from France of the vast American territory known as Louisiana. The success of this mission showed Monroe to be a skillful diplomat. After that, he served as minister to Great Britain, as governor of Virginia for a second time, and as secretary of state, when he tried to reach agreement with Britain over the impressment of American seamen. He soon saw that war was inevitable. During the War of 1812, he held the office of Secretary of State and Secretary of War simultaneously. In 1816, Monroe was elected President of the United States.

Monroe became President at a time when industry was beginning to flourish in the Northern states, and new frontiers were being carved out in the West. It was a peaceful and prosperous time for the country. No bitter political fights were taking place, and the country was expanding to the West.

James Monroe was a likeable gentleman, whose years in the Presidency were called the "Era of Good Feelings." But an important issue arose near the end of his first administration—the question of slavery. The country was becoming divided over this question. Monroe privately agreed with the slaveowners, but his chief aim was to keep the country united. In 1820, he agreed to the so-called Missouri Compromise. This agreement, made in Congress, allowed slavery in the new state of Missouri, but forbade it in any other part of Louisiana Territory. During this time, the United States borders were extended to the south, after the purchase of Florida from Spain in 1819.

In 1820, Monroe ran for reelection with no opponents. During his second term, the attention of most Americans was turned to the revolutionary wars in South America. It was then that Monroe issued his famous warning to European nations—the Monroe Doctrine.

Monroe's Presidency ended in

1825, and he retired to his estate of Oak Hill in Virginia. After his wife died, he spent his last year with his daughter in New York City.

ALSO READ: LOUISIANA PURCHASE, MISSOURI, MONROE DOCTRINE, SLAVERY, WAR OF 1812.

MONROE DOCTRINE On December 2, 1823, President James Monroe sent a message to Congress stating that the continents of North and South America shall never again "be considered as subjects for future colonization by any European powers." He also made it clear that the United States would consider any attempt by European nations to interfere in the affairs of any country of the Western Hemisphere as a direct threat to the peace and safety of the United States.

In 1815, the leaders of Russia, Austria, and Prussia had joined in what was called a "Holy Alliance." President Monroe believed that the Holy Alliance would support Spain's efforts to regain control of its former South America colonies. His message to Congress was a warning to the European nations that the United States would come to the aid of any other country in the Western Hemisphere.

The Monroe Doctrine, worked out by Secretary of State John Quincy Adams, was later regarded unfavorably by Latin American countries. They felt that it meant the United States could interfere in their affairs. In the 1920's and 1930's, Presidents Hoover and Roosevelt added the idea of the "Good Neighbor Policy" to the Monroe Doctrine. This meant that the United States would not interfere in Latin American politics—just as Europe had been told not to interfere before.

ALSO READ: COLONY; INTERNATIONAL RELATIONS; MONROE, JAMES.

MONSOON The word "monsoon" comes from the Arabic word for "season." A monsoon is a wind that blows from land to sea during one season (winter), and from sea to land during another season (summer), mainly in southern Asia.

Monsoons are caused by differences in temperature between the land and sea. During the summer, the earth takes in a lot of heat from the summer sun, warming the air above the land. When the summer monsoons blow, cool air from over the sea blows toward the land. This cool air also carries moisture from the sea, and rain falls over the land. Summer monsoons are called "wet monsoons." Summer monsoons bring the "rainy season." For example, Allahabad, India, and Washington, D.C., get the same amount of rainfall over a full year. In Washington, rain falls equally throughout the year. But in Allahabad, most of the rain falls during the summer monsoons—in June, July, August, and September.

During the winter, the land grows cooler that the sea. The cool air then blows from the land toward the sea. Winter monsoons are called "dry monsoons." In China, the winter monsoon brings dust storms. The air blowing to the sea carries yellowish dust from the dry land. The dust fills

Since ancient times sailors have used the seasonal turn around of the monsoon winds on their voyages. Sailing ships in the Arabian Sea sail westward from India to Africa when the monsoon blows toward the southwest. In summer, the monsoon blows from the southwest and the trading vessels return to India.

▼ *The monsoon season in India, showing the concentration of rainfall in the months between June and October.*

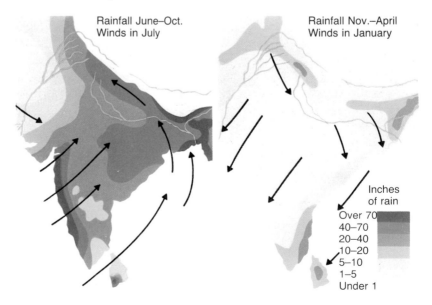

Rainfall June–Oct.
Winds in July

Rainfall Nov.–April
Winds in January

Inches
of rain
Over 70
40–70
20–40
10–20
5–10
1–5
Under 1

▲ *Families wade through the flooded streets of a refugee camp in Madras, India, after the heavy monsoon rains.*

the air for weeks at a time sifting through windows, covering everything. Chinese farmers have been known to attach sails to wheelbarrows for the monsoon to push.

ALSO READ: WEATHER, WIND.

MONTANA The name "Montana" comes from a Spanish word meaning "mountainous." Western Montana is a very mountainous region that contains Glacier National Park. The park is one of the places where you can see the Rocky Mountains at their best. It is a wilderness of steep, wooded slopes and flowery mountain meadows. Streams tumble over waterfalls. Blue lakes lie in peaceful valleys. High in the mountains are *glaciers*. A glacier is a great sheet of ice that moves slowly down a slope or valley. Glacier National Park has more than 60 glaciers. This park was established in 1910 and contains 1,031,129 acres (417,298 hectares).

The park has other wonders, too. One of them is Triple Divide Peak. This mountain rises about 1½ miles (2.4 km) above sea level. Its name gives you a hint as to what makes it unusual. The streams that run down its slopes flow in three directions. On the western side, the water drains into rivers bound for the Pacific Ocean. On the eastern side, some water flows north, finally to reach the cold

Look at the map of Montana. Does the state's western border look like the profile of a man's face? Some people say it looks something like former President Richard Nixon.

Hudson Bay in Canada. The water that flows south ends up in the warm Gulf of Mexico.

The Land and Climate Triple Divide Park stands on the Continental Divide, the high ridges of the Rocky Mountains. The Rockies cover the western two-fifths of Montana. They spread into Idaho on the west and southwest and into Wyoming in the south. Montana's northern Rockies extend into Canada. Across the border from Glacier National Park is Canada's Waterton Lakes National Park. Together, the two form the International Peace Park.

East of the Rockies in Montana lie the Great Plains. These rolling plains span the Canadian border in the north and the Wyoming border in the south. They are highest at the foot of the Rockies. They slope downward into North Dakota in the east. The plains are dotted with hills and crossed by rivers. Most of these rivers flow into the Missouri River.

Winters can be very cold in Montana. You would expect the high mountains to be cold, but the plains are too. Icy winds from Canada sweep across them. These winds often bring blizzards. A warm, dry wind called a *chinook* sometimes blows down the

▼ *Visitors to the Lewis and Clark Caverns near Whitehall, Montana, find a fascinating growth of stalagmites and stalactites.*

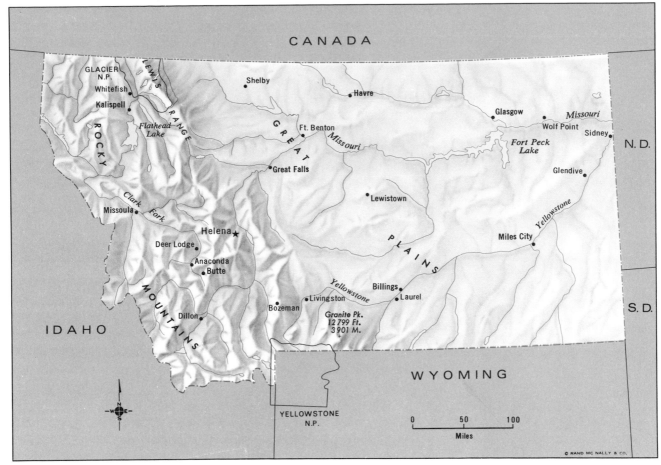

MONTANA

Capital
Helena (25,800 people)

Area
147,138 square miles
(381,058 sq. km)
Rank: 4th

Population
807,000 people
Rank: 44th

Statehood
November 8, 1889
(41st state admitted)

Principal rivers
Missouri River
Yellowstone River

Highest point
Granite Peak;
12,799 feet (3,901 m)

Largest city
Billings (69,000 people)

Motto
Oro y Plata (Gold and Silver)

Song
"Montana"

Famous people
Gary Cooper, Will James,
Myrna Loy, Mike Mansfield,
Jeannette Rankin

STATE EMBLEMS

Ponderosa Pine

Bitterroot

Western Meadowlark

Other than Alaska and Wyoming, Montana has fewer people per square mile than any other state—5.7 (2.2 per square km).

eastern slopes of the Rockies. The temperatures can suddenly rise more than 50° F (30° C)! Chinooks make the winter weather suddenly milder and often melt away snow. Summers are cool and pleasant in Montana's mountains, but hot in the plains.

Precipitation is generally light throughout the state. The mountains have enough moisture for trees to grow. But the plains are much drier. The chief vegetation on the plains is grass. It grows in bunches on the bare earth. Except in late spring, the grass is more yellow than green.

History The Indians had Montana completely to themselves before 1700. The Flathead Indians lived in the western mountain valleys. The Blackfoot and Crow tribes held most of the plains area. The Flatheads hunted deer and elk in the mountains. They trapped otters and other fur-bearing animals and fished for trout in the rivers and lakes. The plains Indians hunted buffalo (bison). They hunted on foot before white men brought horses to North America. Buffalo meat was the main food of these Indians. They made clothing and *tipis* (tents) from buffalo hides.

The first white people in Montana were French. They came from New France (French Canada) about 1740. Most of Montana was sold to the United States by France as part of the Louisiana Purchase in 1803. An American party led by Meriwether

Lewis and William Clark was then sent to explore the area. These men traveled up the Missouri River to Montana in 1804. They were on their way to the Pacific. Clark explored the Yellowstone River on the return trip. Lewis and Clark returned to St. Louis, Missouri, in 1806. People there were greatly interested in what the explorers said about the unknown West. A Missouri fur trader named Manuel Lisa was especially interested. He took some men up the Yellowstone River in 1807 and built Montana's first trading post at the point where the Bighorn River meets the Yellowstone. The fur trade was Montana's earliest industry.

A priest-pioneer arrived in the region in 1840. He was Father Pierre Jean de Smet from Belgium. He and several other priests founded a mission in the valley of the Bitterroot River. The priests taught the Flathead Indians about Christianity and also taught them European farming methods. The first crops grown in Montana in the white people's way were the potatoes, wheat, and oats planted at the mission.

Gold was discovered at Grasshopper Creek in southwestern Montana during the Civil War. Miners rushed there and took out ten million dollars' worth of gold in a single year. This was the beginning of Montana's mining industry. Silver was found north of the gold region in 1875. The city of Butte sprang up near the gold mines. Later, silver and copper were discovered there.

The Wild West was truly wild in those days. Robbings and killings were common in Montana.

Indians became alarmed as more and more white people arrived. They feared the loss of their hunting grounds. Some tribes fought the settlers and the United States Army in the 1870's. General George Custer and his entire command of 265 soldiers were killed at the Little Big Horn River on June 25, 1876. The

▼ *Montana's grasslands are good for grazing cattle. Clear streams, such as this one near Ronan, attract many trout fishermen. In the background can be seen the spectacular Mission Range.*

▲ *The sheer cliffs at Devil Canyon, seen from the overlook at Big Horn Canyon.*

Indians won many battles, but they lost the war to the whites. They were forced to live on reservations. There are now Blackfeet, Crow, Sioux and Cheyenne settled on seven reservations.

As more people came to Montana, the need for food increased. Soon the grass that had fed the buffalo was feeding cattle and sheep. Crops were planted in mountain valleys and on the plains.

Montana at Work Today, agriculture is Montana's most important business. Cattle raising is still widespread. Much of Montana's farming is carried on by irrigation in river valleys. But the leading crop, wheat, is raised by a method called *dry farming*. Wheat farmers raise a crop only every second year. Moisture builds up in the soil, and the farmers can use two years' rain to grow one year's crop.

Manufacturing is the state's second largest business. Timber from mountain forests provides raw material for the state's chief product—lumber. Farm products are processed into sugar, flour, and meal. The third

biggest business is mining. Oil, copper, and coal now earn the most money in this industry. Tourism is also an important source of income and is growing rapidly. Camping, fishing, hunting, horseback riding, mountain climbing, and skiing are available. People can tour mines near Butte and visit Indian reservations.

ALSO READ: BISON; BLACKFOOT INDIANS; CUSTER, GEORGE; FUR; GLACIER; LEWIS AND CLARK EXPEDITION.

MONTH Our calendar, the system we use to tell the time of year, is made up of days, weeks, months, and years. Originally, a month was the period between one new moon and another, about 29½ days. This is a *lunar month*. The word "month" comes from *moon*.

Our months vary from 28 to 31 days each. Every four years an extra day is added to February to make our calendar fit the solar calendar. (The amount of time it takes the Earth to go all the way around the sun is 365¼ days.) The calendar of the ancient Egyptians had 12 months of 30 days each. The first Roman calendar had only ten months and began with *Martius* (March), named for Mars, god of war. Then came *Aprilis* (April), from the Latin "aperire," "to open"; *Maius* (May), probably from Maia, goddess of spring; and *Iunius* (June), maybe from Juno, goddess of marriage. The other Roman months received their names from the Latin numbers five through ten. *Quintilis*, the fifth month, was changed to *Julius* (July), in honor of Julius Caesar; and *Sextilis*, to *Augustus* (August), in honor of Augustus Caesar. The Romans later added *Ianuarius* (January), named for Janus, a god whose two faces looked backward and forward; and *Februarius* (February), from the Latin "februare," "to purify." The calendar used today is based on the Roman model.

The average length of a *lunar* month is 29 days, 12 hours, 44 minutes, and 2.8 seconds. The moon travels around the Earth in 27 days, 7 hours, 43 minutes, and 11.5 seconds. This is called the *sidereal* month.

▼ *The calendar we use today is based on the ancient Roman calendar. The emperor Julius Caesar (below) gave his name to our seventh month, July.*

In 1968, it was discovered that a satellite's orbit was changed as it passed over some points on the moon's surface. Scientists think that there are large chunks of heavy material in these regions, which change the gravity of the moon at these points. The regions occur underneath the lunar "seas."

The French Revolutionary calendar, used in France from 1793 to 1805, had "seasonal" names for the 12 months. These names were vintage, fog, sleet, snow, rain, wind, seed, blossom, pasture, harvest, heat, and fruit.

ALSO READ: CALENDAR, MOON; *see articles on each month.*

MONTICELLO see JEFFERSON, THOMAS.

MONTREAL The first European to visit the site of present-day Montreal, Canada, was a Frenchman, Jacques Cartier. In 1535, Cartier explored an island inhabited by more than 1,000 Indians, who welcomed him warmly. He named a mountain on the island "Mont Réal" (Mount Royal). The modern city of Montreal, located on the St. Lawrence River in southern Quebec, is built around Mount Royal. Twelve bridges span the river to connect Montreal with the mainland.

A hundred years passed after Cartier's visit before Montreal was permanently settled by the French. Development of the settlement was greatly hindered by frequent Indian attacks. During the 1700's the town grew and became a center of the fur trade. In

▼ *Modern skyscrapers dominate the Montreal skyline and at night present a spectacular sight with their lights ablaze.*

1760, Montreal was captured by the British.

Today, Montreal is the largest city (in population) in Canada and the second largest French-speaking city in the world. (Paris is first.) Over three million people live in and around Montreal. About two-thirds of the city's people are of French descent. Both French and English are spoken.

Montreal is a city of great contrasts with modern skyscrapers and rows of very old houses, some of which date from the period of the French occupation. Oil refining and food processing (canned goods, sugar, and beer) are the leading industries. Much clothing, transportation equipment, electrical machinery, steel, and plastics are manufactured in Montreal. The city has a fine subway (the Métro), a large international airport (opened in 1975), a renowned symphony orchestra, outstanding museums and universities, and professional hockey, football, and baseball teams. Montreal was the site of the Olympic Games in the summer of 1976.

ALSO READ: CANADA, QUEBEC.

MOON When Neil Armstrong and Edwin Aldrin stepped onto the surface of the moon on July 20, 1969, they were fulfilling an ancient dream of a voyage to the moon. The moon has been a source of wonder—and fear—for thousands of years. A *lunar eclipse* (when the Earth is directly between the moon and the sun) and a *solar eclipse* (when the moon is directly between the Earth and the sun) often frightened people who did not understand what was happening. But people have learned a great deal about the moon, both from what they have seen through giant telescopes and from information brought back by spacecraft and samples collected by the Apollo 11 astronauts.

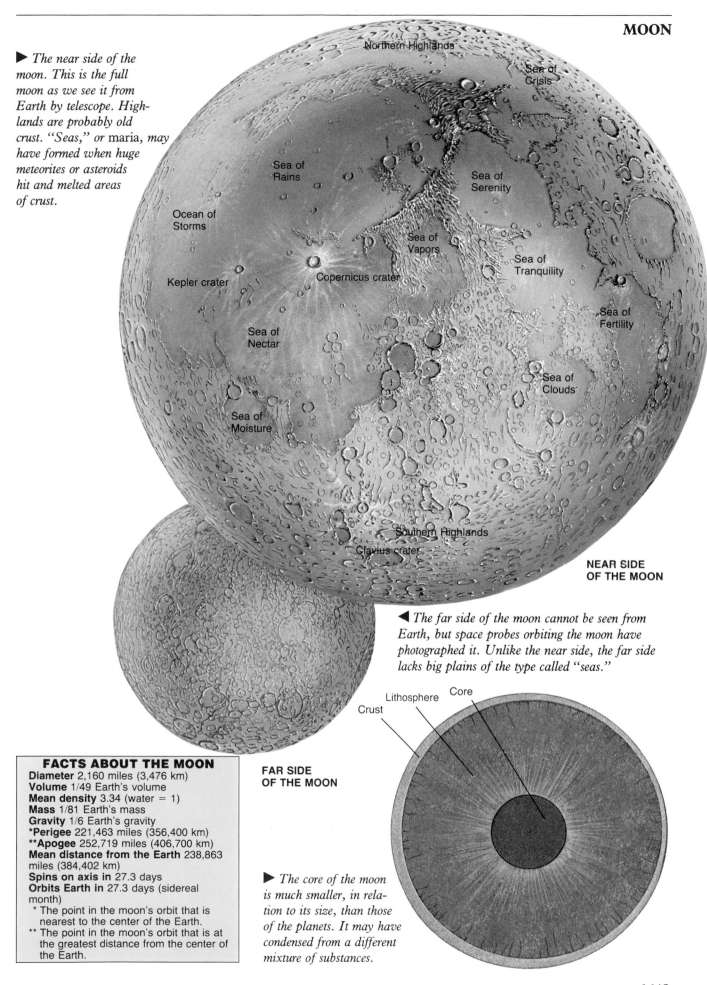

▶ *The near side of the moon. This is the full moon as we see it from Earth by telescope. Highlands are probably old crust. "Seas," or* maria, *may have formed when huge meteorites or asteroids hit and melted areas of crust.*

Northern Highlands

Sea of Crisis

Sea of Rains

Sea of Serenity

Ocean of Storms

Sea of Vapors

Kepler crater

Sea of Tranquility

Copernicus crater

Sea of Fertility

Sea of Nectar

Sea of Clouds

Sea of Moisture

Southern Highlands

Clavius crater

NEAR SIDE OF THE MOON

◀ *The far side of the moon cannot be seen from Earth, but space probes orbiting the moon have photographed it. Unlike the near side, the far side lacks big plains of the type called "seas."*

Lithosphere   Core
Crust
FAR SIDE OF THE MOON

FACTS ABOUT THE MOON
Diameter 2,160 miles (3,476 km)
Volume 1/49 Earth's volume
Mean density 3.34 (water = 1)
Mass 1/81 Earth's mass
Gravity 1/6 Earth's gravity
***Perigee** 221,463 miles (356,400 km)
****Apogee** 252,719 miles (406,700 km)
Mean distance from the Earth 238,863 miles (384,402 km)
Spins on axis in 27.3 days
Orbits Earth in 27.3 days (sidereal month)
 * The point in the moon's orbit that is nearest to the center of the Earth.
 ** The point in the moon's orbit that is at the greatest distance from the center of the Earth.

▶ *The core of the moon is much smaller, in relation to its size, than those of the planets. It may have condensed from a different mixture of substances.*

▲ *Edwin Aldrin, the second man on the moon, photographed by the first: Neil Armstrong. Armstrong and the lunar module* Eagle *are reflected in Aldrin's visor.*

When scientists dated a piece of moon rock brought back by the Apollo 12 astronauts they found it to be 4.6 billion years old. This makes it the oldest rock yet found on the moon or on Earth. It is thought that the Earth was formed about 5 billion years ago.

Origin of the Moon Most of the planets in our solar system have satellites—smaller bodies that maintain a constant orbit around them. Some planets have several satellites. Mercury, Venus, and Pluto have none. The Earth has only one natural satellite—the moon. There are several theories (ideas) about the origin of the moon. The most widely held theory is that the moon was formed from the same nebula (gas cloud) that formed the sun, the Earth, and the other planets and their moons. As the gas cloud grew smaller, particles constantly collided and clung together to form the planets and their satellites. Other scientists believe that the moon once had its own orbit around the sun. It came within the Earth's gravitational range and was pulled out of its orbit around the sun to circle the Earth.

Some scientists once believed that the moon was once a part of the Earth and became separated during the Earth's formation by our planet's rapid rotation. They thought that the hole left by the moon was the bed of the Pacific Ocean—which was later filled with water. This theory was proved to be incorrect after examination of moon rocks brought back by astronauts. Moon rocks have large amounts of minerals that are rare on the Earth—indicating that the moon was probably never a part of the Earth.

Orbit of the Moon The moon revolves around the Earth in a slightly elliptical (football-shaped) orbit. Its distance from the Earth varies, averaging about 239,000 miles (384,620 km). One revolution of the moon around the Earth takes about 27 days. This is its *sidereal period*. Because the

▶ *A view of the far side of the moon, taken from an orbiting spacecraft. The larger crater is about 50 miles (80 km) across. Like many large craters, it contains a group of mountains.*

Earth revolves around the sun, it takes about 29 days for the moon to revolve and return to a position directly between the Earth and the sun—its *synodic period*. One revolution of the moon is about one Earth month.

The moon completes one revolution about the Earth in the same period of time it takes to complete one rotation about its own axis. As a result, about half of the moon's surface is never turned toward the Earth. This unseen surface has often been called "the dark side of the moon." But all sides of the moon get sunlight for two weeks each month. Recent photographs taken from manned and unmanned spacecraft circling the moon have given scientists information about this dark side. The surface of the dark side is slightly different from the visible side. It has fewer of the big flat areas called *maria*. Maria means "seas," and these flat areas were so named because early astronomers thought they were seas.

Surface of the Moon The Earth's moon is almost perfectly round and

about one-fourth the size of the Earth. Its surface is covered with thousands of deep, wide pits, or *craters*, which may be up to 300 miles (480 km) across. There are often tall mountain peaks in the centers of the craters. Scientists have different opinions about the origin of these craters. Some believe that they were formed by meteors crashing into the moon. Others believe that the peaks were once explosive volcanoes. When the volcanoes erupted, the explosions hollowed out the areas around them, forming the craters. Other areas, including the *maria*, are fairly flat.

GRAVITY AND TEMPERATURE. The moon has no atmosphere. The gravity on the moon's surface is too weak to prevent the escape of gases into space. The moon's gravitational pull is only one-sixth that of the Earth. A person who weighs 200 pounds (90 kg) on Earth would only weigh about 33 pounds (15 kg) on the moon!

The temperature on the moon varies greatly. It might be 300° F (150° C) during the "lunar day" (where the sun's rays light the surface) and 180° F below zero (−118° C) at "lunar

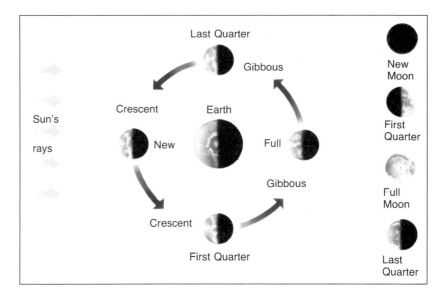

night" (where the surface is in darkness). Two factors cause these wide differences in temperature. When the sun's rays hit the moon, there is no atmospheric blanket to absorb much of the heat before it reaches the surface, causing the "lunar day" to be extremely hot. But the surface material of the moon does not hold in most of the "daylight" heat, causing the moon to be extremely cold when it is in darkness.

Phases of the Moon The moon gives off no light of its own. It simply reflects the light from the sun. Only the section reflecting the sun's light can be seen from the Earth. The positions of the Earth, sun, and moon as the Earth orbits the sun and the moon orbits the Earth affect the amount of light reflected by the moon, changing its appearance during each month. These changes in appearance are the *phases* of the moon.

There are four main phases of the moon. When the moon is between the Earth and the sun, and the moon's face is completely shadowed, it is called the *new moon*. Just before and just after the new moon, a thin *crescent* (C-shaped) moon appears. After the new moon, the crescent appears on the eastern side of the moon. Each night, the crescent gets a little larger.

▲ *The moon shows phases because the sun can illuminate only one hemisphere. It rotates once on its axis during the lunar month, therefore always keeping the same face toward the Earth.*

How big do you think the moon is? It is probably smaller than you think. It is 2,160 miles (3,476 km) across, which is less than the width of the United States.

If the Earth were a tennis ball, the moon would be the size of a marble about 6½ feet (2 m) away.

▲ *A piece of rock from the surface of the moon, brought back by Apollo astronauts. Its age, estimated at 4,600 million years, indicates that it was formed very early in the moon's history.*

▲ *Thomas More, English statesman, writer, and saint.*

Thomas More named his book *Utopia* from two Greek words, *ou* and *topos*, which mean "not" and "place"—nowhere. Today, when people use the word utopia, they mean a place or situation where everything is impossibly ideal.

When the entire eastern half of the moon is visible, the moon is in its *first quarter*. When the entire face of the moon is lit, the phase is called the *full moon*. The moon is in its *last quarter* when only the entire western half is lit.

Modern-day science has proved that ancient people were not completely wrong in their belief that the moon has tremendous influence on human beings, on some biological processes, and on the planet Earth.

The moon's greatest influence is on tides. The gravitational pull of the moon causes the tides to rise and fall all over the Earth. There seems no limit to the knowledge that people may receive about the universe from exploring this "new frontier"—the moon.

ALSO READ: ALDRIN, EDWIN; ARMSTRONG, NEIL; ASTRONOMY; EARTH HISTORY; ECLIPSE; METEOR; SATELLITE; SOLAR SYSTEM; SPACE RESEARCH; SPACE TRAVEL; TELESCOPE; TIDE; UNIVERSE.

MORE, SIR THOMAS (1478–1535) Sir Thomas More was an English statesman and lawyer. He was also the author of a book called *Utopia.* Utopia was the name he gave to an imaginary island in the middle of the ocean. There was no crime in Utopia, and there were no poor or hungry people. Everyone was equal, and worked at the job he or she did best. The happy island of Utopia was very different from the court of King Henry VIII, where More served as lord chancellor (chief minister) of England. He was the most important person in the kingdom, next to the king.

While More was lord chancellor, King Henry decided to divorce his wife, Catherine of Aragon, and marry a lady of the court, Anne Boleyn. Pope Clement VII forbade the divorce because it was against the laws of the Roman Catholic Church. More did not support King Henry's plan of divorce and, claiming ill health, resigned as lord chancellor.

Later, More refused to sign King Henry's Oath of Supremacy, which stated that the king, not the pope, was the leader of the Church of England. More was imprisoned in the Tower of London. He was convicted of high treason and beheaded on July 6, 1535. In 1935, Pope Pius XI declared More a saint.

ALSO READ: ENGLISH HISTORY; HENRY, KINGS OF ENGLAND.

MORGAN, SIR HENRY see PIRATES AND PRIVATEERS.

MORMON see ILLINOIS, LATTER-DAY SAINTS, UTAH.

MOROCCO Morocco has the broadest plains and the tallest mountains in North Africa. It lies on the northwest coast of Africa. The port of Tangier is on the Strait of Gibraltar, the narrow channel between the Atlantic Ocean and the Mediterranean Sea. Morocco's west coast is on the Atlantic, and on the north it borders the Mediterranean. It is bounded on the east and southeast by Algeria, and on the south by the Western Sahara. (See the map with the article on AFRICA.)

The rugged Atlas Mountains rise to a height of over 13,000 feet (3,900 m) in Morocco. An area of highlands called Er Rif parallels the Mediterranean coast. Most Moroccans live in the Atlantic coastal plain, where rainfall provides a water supply. Here are located Rabat, the capital, and Casablanca, the largest city and main seaport. Two historic cities are found inland near the mountains—Fez, containing a Muslim university more than 1,000 years old, and Marrakech, famous for its leather goods.

MOROCCO

Capital City: Rabat (568,000 people).

Area: 172,414 square miles (446,518 sq. km).

Population: 25,906,000.

Government: Monarchy.

Natural Resources: Phosphates, iron ore, manganese, lead, zinc.

Export Products: Food and beverages, semi-processed foods, consumer goods, phosphates.

Unit of Money: Dirham.

Official Language: Arabic.

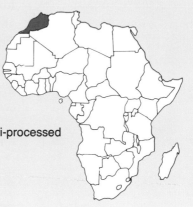

Farming is the mainstay of the Moroccan economy, although less than 20 percent of Morocco can be cultivated. Wheat and barley are the leading crops. Corn, beans, peas, and grapes are also grown. Orange, lemon, and almond trees and date palms grow well in the warm climate. Phosphates are mined and exported. Other minerals are ores of iron, manganese, zinc, lead, and cobalt, and anthracite coal. Cork oak, evergreen oak, juniper, cedar, fir, and pine grow in the millions of acres of forest.

Morocco's chief industries include food processing, leather tanning, and the manufacture of textiles, chemicals, and cement. Hydroelectric plants supply the country's power.

Bedouin Arabs make up the majority of the population in Morocco. The Berbers, who at one time ruled most of northwest Africa, live in isolated villages in the high mountain areas. The history of Morocco has been shaped by the original Berber people and various foreign invaders.

The first known foreign invaders were the Phoenicians, who in the 1100's B.C. established trading posts on the Mediterranean coast. Carthage and then Rome conquered the area. After a period of Vandal and Byzantine Christian rule, the Arabs conquered Morocco in A.D. 682 when they invaded the region to spread the religion of Islam. In 1212, the large Muslim empire fell to Spain.

In 1415, Portugal captured Moroccan ports, but the Moors (Spanish Muslims) later defeated Portugal. Germany, France, and Spain became rivals over control of Morocco. In 1904, Morocco was divided into French and Spanish protectorates. France and Spain recognized Moroccan independence in 1956.

Morocco is a constitutional monarchy with a unicameral legislature and a king as head of state. Since 1979, Morocco has occupied the Western Sahara region. But many Saharans support a group called the Polisario Front, which opposes Moroccan rule. Fighting between Morocco and the Polisario Front continued into the late 1980's.

ALSO READ: AFRICA, BARBARY COAST, BYZANTINE EMPIRE, MEDITERRANEAN SEA.

Casablanca, the biggest town in Morocco, has many white buildings in it. The name "casa blanca" means "white house" in Spanish. The town grew up around a small Arab village, now called the Old Medina.

▼ *Women in a market in Morocco display their produce to sell. For many Muslim women, modesty dictates that they dress to cover themselves completely.*

▲ *Samuel F. B. Morse, American artist and inventor.*

In 1912, a Morse code message helped save the lives of some of the passengers on the sinking ship *Titanic*. A telegraph operator in New York picked up the ship's SOS signal and directed rescuers to the doomed ocean liner.

MORSE, SAMUEL F. B. (1791–1872) Samuel Finley Breese Morse was an American inventor and artist. He designed the first telegraph powerful enough to send signals over long distances. In order that messages could be sent over the telegraph, Morse invented the system later known as the "Morse code."

Samuel Morse was born in Charlestown, Massachusetts. As a young man, he wanted to be an artist. He studied art at Yale University and at the Royal Academy of Arts in London, England. When Morse returned from London, his greatest ambition was to paint large historical paintings for the United States Capitol, then being built in Washington, D.C. He traveled to Europe again to prepare for the possibility of working on the Capitol. When Morse was returning from Europe in 1832, he met a man who talked about the possibility of sending a signal over an electric wire. Morse became very interested in this invention.

When he did not receive a commission to paint the Capitol paintings, he began to experiment with electrical machines. He believed that electricity could be used to send messages over wires for long distances. He worked on this project for ten years, living close to poverty. He taught art to pay for his research.

Morse's first attempt to make a long-distance system ended in disaster. He stretched a wire from Manhattan across New York Harbor to Governors Island. But a ship's anchor broke the wire, and the people who had come to see the demonstration left angrily.

In 1843, Congress finally gave Morse the money he needed to test the telegraph. He set up a telegraph wire from Washington, D.C., to Baltimore. While members of Congress watched, he sent the Morse code message, "What hath God wrought." It was received at the other end of the line, 50 miles (80 km) away. Morse became an immediate success. Telegraph companies were soon set up in the United States and Europe.

ALSO READ: COMMUNICATION, MORSE CODE, TELEGRAPH.

▶ *A diagram of Morse's electric telegraph system (1882). From the 1770's there were many experiments with telegraph systems. But Morse invented a code to translate messages over the wires that was simple to use, and so his method was adopted.*

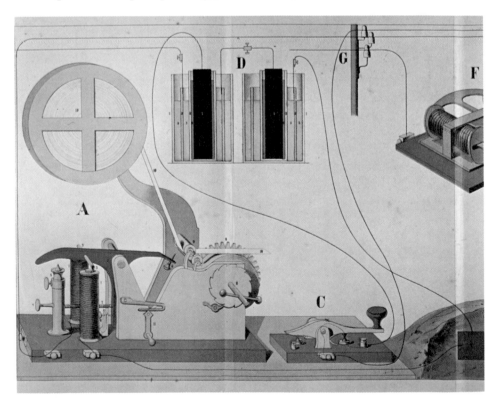

MORSE CODE The Morse code is a system of dots and dashes used to send messages by telegraph wire. The code was named after its inventor, Samuel F. B. Morse. You can see the code on the right-hand side of this page.

Morse code was an important way to send messages before the telephone and radio were invented. If you send a telegram today, it might still be sent by Morse code. But most telegrams are now sent by a machine called a *teletype*, which converts a special code directly into printed letters.

The dots and dashes of the Morse code are based on timing. The dot is a rapid click. A short dash sounds twice as long as a dot. Each letter of the alphabet is represented by a different combination of dots and dashes. The code also includes numerals and punctuation marks. A space between words is as long as six dots. The telegraph operator "taps" out the message by pressing and releasing a special telegraph key. When he or she presses down the key, an electrical *impulse,* or signal, is sent over the telegraph wire. At the other end, an instrument called a *receiver* registers the length of each impulse by a buzzing sound—short for a dot and long for a dash. Messages in Morse code are sent over radio waves. A simplified version of the original Morse code, called the *international Morse code*, is used for radio transmission. Only the short dash and dot are used.

ALSO READ: MORSE, SAMUEL F. B.; RADIO; SIGNAL; TELECOMMUNICATIONS; TELEGRAPH.

MOSAIC For more than 2,000 years, people have created mosaics to decorate the walls, floors, and ceilings of buildings. Mosaics are designs made by fitting together small pieces of hard, colored material. The small pieces are called *tesserae*. Tesserae can be any shape. Marble, glass, tile, pebbles, shells, and even seeds are used as tesserae. Marble and tile are usually used for floor mosaics. Glass and the more breakable materials are used for mosaics on walls, ceilings, tabletops, and other surfaces.

The ancient Egyptians made brightly colored mosaics showing plants and animals. The ancient Greeks and especially the Romans created very complicated floor mosaics using marble tesserae. Many mosaics were discovered in the Roman city of Pompeii. It was covered over by volcanic lava from the eruption of Mount Vesuvius in about A.D. 79. The Pompeiian mosaic here shows four musicians. Look closely, and you can see how the artist used lighter and darker tesserae to make shading for the shadows on the floor and wall, the folds of the garments, and the roundness of the body parts. The mosaic is almost like a painting.

During the Byzantine period in art (A.D. 330–1453), mosaics became one of the most widely used decorations in churches and cathedrals. The Byzantine artists used glass tesserae. Glass is shinier than marble, and light reflects from it. So the tesserae seem to glitter.

Compare the Byzantine mosaic of Christ and the Virgin Mary with the Roman mosaic of the musicians. You can see that the colors of the Byzan-

International Morse Code	
a · −	y − · − −
b − · · ·	z − − · ·
c − · − ·	
d − · ·	1 · − − − −
e ·	2 · · − − −
f · · − ·	3 · · · − −
g − − ·	4 · · · · −
h · · · ·	5 · · · · ·
i · ·	6 − · · · ·
j · − − −	7 − − · · ·
k − · −	8 − − − · ·
l · − · ·	9 − − − − ·
m − −	0 − − − − −
n − ·	
o − − −	(.) · · · · · ·
p · − − ·	(,) − − · · − −
q − − · −	(;) − · − · − ·
r · − ·	(:) − − − · · ·
s · · ·	(!) − − · · − −
t −	(?) · · − − · ·
u · · −	start − · −
v · · · −	end · − · − ·
w · − −	wait · − · · ·
x − · · −	sos · · · − − − · · ·

▲ *The famous dots and dashes of the Morse code.*

▼ *The finest houses in Pompeii were decorated with marble mosaics. Some of the mosaics had a light and humorous theme, such as this one of a group of dancing musicians.*

▲ *This mosaic floor from ancient Greece shows the god Dionysus riding a panther. It dates from the end of the 300's* B.C. *Mosaics made from natural colored pebbles, such as this, have been traced as far back as the 400's* B.C.

The world's largest mosaic adorns four walls in the National University, in Mexico City. It shows historical scenes. The two largest mosaic-covered walls are 13,000 square feet (1,200 sq. m) in area.

tine mosaic are sharp and bright, while the Roman colors are soft. The Byzantine mosaic contains a great deal of gold, but the Roman mosaic has none. With marble tesserae, the artist can use only the natural colors of marble. There is no gold marble, but glass can be tinted with gold or any color the artist chooses. Byzantine artists used a lot of gold in their religious mosaics. That color seemed to give a feeling of the greatness of God.

The human figures in Byzantine mosaics are "stiffer" than in Roman mosaics. The Byzantine artists did not try to make their religious figures look real. The artists wanted them to look like people from heaven—different from ordinary human beings. Look closely at the tesserae in the clothing of the Byzantine figures. You can see that the pieces of glass are like a design. The colors are arranged in stripes that move in various directions. The draped clothing of the Virgin Mary, as well as the main facial features, are outlined in a darker color. Outlining makes the figures look stiffer than those in the Roman mosaic, where no outlining is used. The

Roman figures are natural looking.

In Central and South America, Inca, Aztec, and Maya artists created designs in stone mosaics to decorate their places of worship. Artists in Persia and India created beautiful glass and tile mosaics. The doorways, domes, and minarets of some Persian mosques are covered entirely with tile mosaics. These are mostly blue, with green, yellow, and orange plantlike decorations and quotations from the Koran, the holy book of Islam containing the sayings of Muhammad.

■ **LEARN BY DOING**

You can make your own mosaic design, using pebbles, seeds, shells, bits of broken china, or small bathroom tiles as tesserae. You will need a square board, or a very stiff piece of cardboard, and some strong glue. Draw your design on the board and decide which colors you will use for each area of the design. Begin gluing the tesserae along the edges first, working inward toward the center. Glue the tesserae as close together as possible. When the glue dries, your mosaic is ready to hang on the wall. If you use tiles or pebbles for tesserae, ask an adult to help you put some

▼ *A mosaic in the church of Santa Prassede in Rome, Italy, shows the Virgin Mary holding the child, Jesus. It is considered one of the best preserved examples of Byzantine art in Rome.*

grout, or filler, in the spaces between the tesserae. Tiles and pebbles are heavy, and the grout will help to hold your mosaic together better than glue alone. ■

ALSO READ: BYZANTINE EMPIRE, POMPEII, ROMANESQUE ART.

◄ *Moscow Underground. The tunnels and approaches of the subway system are unique in their lavish decoration and lighting.*

MOSCOW Moscow is the capital city of Russia. From 1917 to 1991, it was also the capital and largest city of the Union of Soviet Socialist Republics (U.S.S.R.) About nine million people live in Moscow.

Although Moscow lies far inland, it is sometimes referred to as the "Port of Five Seas." Ships from the Baltic, White, Black, and Caspian seas and the Sea of Azov travel to Moscow by way of the Volga-Don and Moscow canals and the Moskva River.

Moscow streets are laid out in rings and semicircles. The *Kremlin* is in the center of the city. The Kremlin Palace is surrounded by a high stone wall. Near it are cathedrals, other palaces and the Bell Tower of Ivan the Great. In front of the Kremlin is Red Square, where parades are held. Facing on the square are the tomb of Nikolai Lenin (founder of the Soviet state), and the Cathedral of St. Basil with its onion-shaped domes.

Moscow has many theaters for drama, ballet, concerts and opera. It has a large university, a library, museums, art galleries, a stadium for sporting events, and many parks.

Moscow is also a manufacturing city. Steel, tools, chemicals, cars, airplanes, furniture, textiles, and many other articles are made there.

The city was founded as a fortified village in the 1100's. Grand Duke Ivan III made Moscow a political capital during his reign (1462–1505). The seat of government was moved to St. Petersburg in 1712.

French troops under Napoleon occupied Moscow in 1812, but soon afterward, a fire believed to have been set by the Russians burned most of the city to the ground. The French, defeated by hunger and cold, retreated from Russia. Moscow was the site of bloody revolutions against the czar in 1905 and 1917. In 1917 the capital was moved back from St. Petersburg, the old czarist capital, to the new Soviet capital of Moscow.

In 1991, many changes occurred in the U.S.S.R. Several Soviet states, including Russia itself, strove for independence. For some it was granted. Moscow is, therefore, no longer such a center of power.

ALSO READ: KREMLIN, RUSSIAN HISTORY, SOVIET UNION.

The famous Red Square in Moscow did not get its name from the Russian Revolution or the Soviet flag. Its name came from the Russian word *krasnya*, which means both red and beautiful. The square has had its name since the Middle Ages.

▼ *The heart of Moscow— Red Square with the walls and turrets of the Kremlin wall on the left, and the domed towers of St. Basil's Cathedral on the right.*

▲ *A mihrab or recess in the 15th century mosque of Sultan Muaiyad in Cairo, Egypt, beautifully decorated in marble.*

▼ *The interior of a mosque in Damascus, Syria. The floor is covered with rugs on which Muslims kneel to pray.*

MOSQUE A mosque is a house of worship for Muslims, people who believe in the religion of Islam. A mosque can be small and simple, but some are magnificent examples of architecture. Most are beautiful, domed buildings, supported by graceful pillars.

Every mosque has certain basic parts. At the entrance is an open courtyard with a fountain or pool, in which people wash themselves before praying. Worshipers pray in a closed meeting room called a *musalla*. Men and women are separated and pray in different parts of the musalla. All face an ornamental *niche* (set-in space) called a *mihrab*. This points the way to Islam's holy city, Mecca. Muslims always pray facing in the direction of Mecca because Muhammad, the chief prophet of the faith of Islam, was born in that city. When Muslims pray, they kneel and bend their heads to the ground and finally lie prostrate, or flat, on the ground. The Koran, the holy book of Islam, is read in the mosque from a pulpit, or platform called the *mimbar*. High above at least one corner of the mosque is a *minaret*, or tower. A man called a *muezzin* climbs up in the tower five times a day to call the faithful to prayer. A religious school may be part of the mosque.

ALSO READ: ISLAM, MUHAMMAD.

▲ *The brightly colored dome of a mosque at Samarra in Iraq.*

MOSQUITO The common name for any of about 2,500 kinds of two-winged flies is "mosquito." The mosquito has a narrow body and long, slender wings. The mouthparts of a mosquito form a hollow, tubelike organ called a *proboscis*, which is not much wider than a hair. The male mosquito uses the proboscis like a straw to feed on plant fluids. Female mosquitoes feed on blood. The proboscis of a female mosquito can pierce the skin of animals.

When a female mosquito "bites," it pushes the proboscis into the victim's skin, probing for a capillary (tiny blood vessel). While biting, the mosquito injects some saliva into the wound. The saliva prevents the blood from clotting and clogging the proboscis. The saliva is what causes the swelling and itching of a mosquito bite.

If a mosquito bites a human being or other animal suffering from a certain disease, the mosquito often carries off disease germs in its saliva. It injects them into the blood of its next victim. In this way, a mosquito may carry such diseases as malaria and yellow fever, often infecting great numbers of people. Fortunately, not all mosquitoes are disease carriers. The common house mosquito is not a carrier of disease.

Female mosquitoes lay their eggs in swamps, marshes, lagoons, and other pools of quiet water. They may lay them in a rain barrel. The larvae are called *wrigglers*, because of their wriggling motion in the water. The pupae are *bullheads*.

People have found that the best way to get rid of mosquitoes is to destroy them while they are in the larva stage. This can be done by pouring a thin layer of oil over the water in which they are growing. The oil prevents air from reaching the larvae, causing them to suffocate. Airplanes have sometimes been used to spray insecticides and other chemicals over bodies of water in regions infested with disease-carrying mosquitoes. If possible, it is best to prevent mosquitoes from breeding at all. This can be done by draining swamps, filling in mud holes, and covering or destroying any containers that can hold water. Rain barrels, for example, are potential breeding places for mosquitoes and should be covered.

ALSO READ: DISEASE, FLY, INSECT.

MOSSES AND LIVERWORTS

Mosses and liverworts are tiny plants that usually live in damp, shady places. They make up the plant group called *Bryophyta*. Mosses and liverworts were two of the first kinds of plants to live on land. Scientists have found traces of these ancient plants. Some are 350 million years old.

Mosses and liverworts grow on soil, rocks, tree bark, and in shallow water. They are hardy plants that live on all the continents of the world. Mosses and liverworts do not have true roots. Instead, they have thread-like growths called *rhizoids*. Rhizoids do two important things that roots do. They absorb water and hold the plant in place. Neither mosses nor liverworts have flowers.

Mosses are small—rarely more than 1½ inches (4 cm) long. Many of them are *evergreen* and grow in both cold and warm weather. The tiny moss plants grow very closely together, forming carpets or pads.

A moss plant reproduces in two stages—*sexual* and *asexual*. The sexual stage involves the joining of male and female sex cells. Some adult plants have capsules containing *sperm*, or male sex cells. Other plants have eggs, or female sex cells. When the sperm capsules ripen and burst open, sperm cells are carried (usually by drops of rain or dew) to egg cells. The

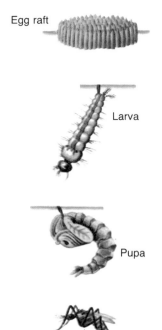

Egg raft

Larva

Pupa

Adult emerging from pupa at surface

▲ *Female mosquitoes lay their eggs on the water surface and the larvae grow up in the water.*

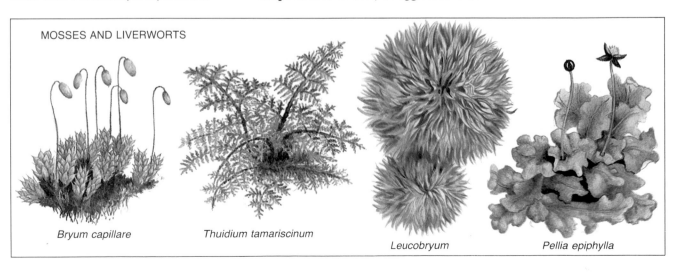

MOSSES AND LIVERWORTS

Bryum capillare   *Thuidium tamariscinum*   *Leucobryum*   *Pellia epiphylla*

In the early days of the West, frontiersmen used to pack the cracks between the logs of their cabins with moss.

sperm unites with, or *fertilizes*, the egg. Then the asexual stage begins. The fertilized egg grows into a stalk with a spore capsule at the end. When the capsule ripens, it bursts open and scatters its spores. These spores grow into new male and female plants.

Mosses are useful in nature because they are among the first plants to grow in barren areas. Their decaying remains form soil in which other plants can grow. *Sphagnum* moss is used as a moisture-holding cover for soil in gardens. It is also sterilized and used in absorbent surgical dressings. Decaying sphagnum forms *peat*, a kind of fuel.

The Lapps used moss for many purposes— they stuffed mattresses with it and lined babies' cradles with it.

Each liverwort plant looks like a tiny leaf. The main body of the plant, the *thallus*, is shaped somewhat like a human liver. This is why the plant is called a liverwort. People once mistakenly believed that liverworts cured liver diseases. Liverworts, like mosses, reproduce in two stages.

ALSO READ: CLUB MOSS, LICHEN, PLANT, PLANT DISTRIBUTION, PLANT KINGDOM, PLANTS OF THE PAST, RE-PRODUCTION.

MOTELS　see HOTELS AND MOTELS.

MOTHER GOOSE　see NURSERY RHYME; PERRAULT, CHARLES.

MOTHS　see BUTTERFLIES AND MOTHS.

MOTION　You watch objects in motion all the time. Tree branches wave in the wind. You and your friends walk home from school. Cars speed past you and high overhead a jet plane zooms across the sky. While all this is going on, the moon is circling the Earth, and the Earth and the other planets are circling the sun.

Nearly all motion—whether the motion is you walking down the street, a river flowing, or the Earth's movement around the sun—is described by three scientific laws. These laws of motion were discovered by Sir Isaac Newton about 300 years ago.

■ **LEARN BY DOING**

Newton's first law says that *an object at rest tends to stay at rest; an object in motion tends to stay in motion*. You can easily do an experiment to show this. You will need a wagon and a board long enough to lay across the top of the wagon.

Put the board on the wagon. Now give the wagon a hard jerk forward. You will yank the wagon right out from under the board. The board— which was at rest—tends to remain at rest.

The opposite is also true. Put the

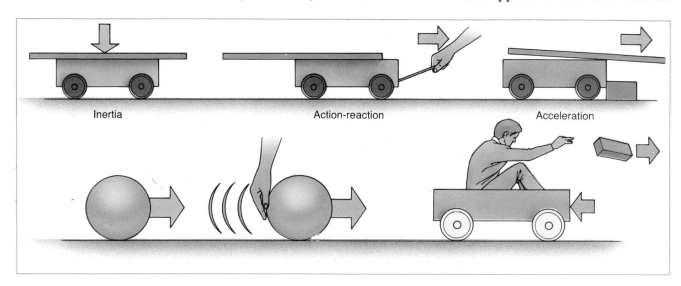

Inertia　　　Action-reaction　　　Acceleration

board back on the wagon. Push the wagon, increasing the speed slowly, so that the board does not get left behind. Then aim the wagon at a curb. When the wagon crashes into the curb, it stops short. But the board keeps moving and flies over the front of the wagon. ■

The tendency all objects have to keep moving—or *not* to move if they are at rest—is called *inertia*. Can you explain how inertia acts on your body when you ride in a car? Why is a seat belt a good idea for automobile passengers?

To make your wagon move, you must push or pull it. A scientist would say you exerted *force* on it. Once it is moving, and if no other forces acted on your wagon, it would roll forever. But on Earth, another force does act on objects. This force is called *friction*. Friction occurs whenever a moving object touches another object. The friction between your wagon wheels and the ground stops your wagon.

Newton's second law explains the changes in motion that force can cause. When a new force is applied to a moving object, what happens depends on two things—the weight of the object and the size of the force.

To measure the speed of a moving object, scientists use *velocity*—how much distance an object moves in a certain amount of time. A turtle's velocity may be 4 inches (10 cm) a minute. A rocket's velocity may be 18,000 miles (29,000 km) an hour.

When a force is applied to an object, the object accelerates. *Acceleration* is the measurement of how quickly velocity changes. When one of your parents steps on the gas pedal in the car, you feel the car accelerating—moving faster and faster.

■ LEARN BY DOING

You can study acceleration. Roll a ball across the floor, and give it a gentle push while it is rolling. What

▲ *To put a motorcycle in motion requires force, supplied by the engine. The capacity of the engine and the weight of the machine and its rider determines the speed at which the motorcycle will go.*

happens? What if you give the ball a hard push? What happens if you push a lightweight ball and a heavy one with equal force? (Try a Ping-Pong ball and a softball.) The heavier the object, the smaller the acceleration. (The balls accelerate only while being pushed, then friction makes them slow down or *decelerate*.)

One other thing—the motion takes place in the direction of the force. What happens if you push a rolling ball from the side? ■

Newton's third law says that for every action, there is an equal but opposite reaction. One example of this is the kind of lawn sprinkler that has spinning arms. As the water squirts, the arms turn in the opposite direction.

■ LEARN BY DOING

Take two or three bricks and sit in a wagon. Throw each brick out as hard as you can. The wagon will roll backward when you throw the bricks forward. This action-reaction explains how a jet engine works, and what makes an inflated balloon soar when released. ■

ALSO READ: ENERGY; FRICTION; JET PROPULSION; NEWTON, SIR ISAAC; PERPETUAL MOTION; ROCKET.

Everything in the whole universe is in motion. As you sit reading this book you are being whirled around with the spinning Earth. The Earth is being whirled around the sun, and the sun itself is moving around the center of the Milky Way galaxy. Even our whole galaxy is shooting through space as the entire universe expands.

▲ *These huge lights are used in making motion pictures to create the right lighting and atmosphere for a particular scene.*

▼ *Both motion pictures and TV rely on a rapid succession of frames. (The TV frames shown here are actually some distance apart.)*

MOTION PICTURE   Motion pictures of one kind or another probably play a big part in your education and entertainment. Perhaps you help your family make home movies. At school you very likely see educational films about history, science, or arithmetic. Many motion pictures are shown on television. Perhaps you even go to a movie theater now and then.

The picture you see on the screen seems to be moving. But you are really seeing a series of pictures flashing one after another, very rapidly. When a motion picture camera is running, the film keeps moving and stopping. Each time it stops the shutter opens briefly and a picture is taken. This happens 24 times a second while the camera is going. Look at 24 pictures on a strip of movie film—one second's worth. You have to look at a hundred frames to see much difference in the pictures. The film is then projected on a screen at the rate of 24 pictures a second, the same speed at which it was photographed. At this speed the human eye sees only a continuously moving picture.

How Motion Pictures Are Made
Thousands of people are needed to make a big feature movie—the kind shown at movie theaters and later on television. But even a simple movie requires the teamwork of a number of people. A *writer* produces the *script*, or story line, of a movie. Sometimes the writer adapts the script from a play or novel. The *producer* selects the script and is in charge of the money. He or she also hires the *director*. Together, the producer and the director select the *cast*, the actors and actresses who will appear in the film. The director tells the cast what to do and the camera people when to start and stop their cameras. *Set designers* build any settings, or background buildings needed for the movie. They also arrange *props*, the furniture and other objects used in the movie. *Costume designers* design and make clothing for the cast to wear in the film. The *makeup* crew applies cosmetics. Sometimes a *composer* writes music to go with the film, and an orchestra plays the music. *Sound recordists* record the music and all sounds made in the film. They make sure that the sound is clear and accurate.

All this work is performed in a motion picture *studio*, or on *location*, when pictures are filmed in a natural setting. A movie about a mountain climber, for instance, might be filmed

▼ *Charlie Chaplin (right), a movie actor known worldwide as a master of comedy, grimaces at an early movie camera.*

▼ *The singer Al Jolson made movie history when he starred in the first "talkie,"* The Jazz Singer, *in 1927.*

in the Rocky Mountains in Wyoming.

A motion picture is not filmed from beginning to end without stopping. Little scenes are shot separately. It may take several weeks and many scenes to film a picture. After all the filming is finished, the *film editor* arranges the hundreds of feet of film taken by the camera people into a smooth-flowing film. The director usually supervises the editing to make sure that the film is put together as he or she wants it.

Early Days of Motion Pictures
People began inventing simple devices to make pictures "move" in the 1800's. An American named Coleman Sellers invented the *kinematoscope* in 1861. This consisted of a series of pictures mounted on a wheel. When the wheel was spun around, the pictures seemed to move. In 1878, a British photographer named Eadweard Muybridge set up 24 cameras at a racetrack. Strings were stretched across the track to the cameras. When a horse raced by, breaking the strings, the cameras recorded the motion of the running horse. The American inventor, Thomas Edison, developed a viewing machine called the *kinetoscope* in 1891. A person who looked through a peephole in the kinetoscope saw a short series of pictures. One showed a person sneezing. Another showed waves rolling to shore. Kinetoscope parlors, the forerunners of movie theaters, were built in New York, Paris, and London. They were tremendously popular.

The first American film to tell a story was *The Great Train Robbery*, produced by Edwin S. Porter in 1903.

The first *nickelodeons* also appeared in 1903. They were gaudy theaters that showed short movies for the price of a nickel. Piano players provided the music. They played fast and loudly during exciting scenes, but gently and sweetly during love scenes. One of the first great American direc-

tors was D. W. Griffith. He produced *The Birth of a Nation* in 1915. Griffith used this Civil War story to try out new camera techniques, such as the *close-up* shot, to make the audience feel more involved in the film.

The Hollywood Era As longer feature films began to be made, large movie houses took the place of nickelodeons. Movies became big business. Small, independent producers were replaced by large production companies, such as Warner Brothers. Many of the large companies established their headquarters in southern California, because the sunny, warm climate there was ideal for moviemaking. Hollywood, California, became "the motion picture capital of the world."

Leading actors and actresses became known as *stars*. The success of a movie began to depend on the popularity of the actor or actress who played the starring role. Each star became known for a particular specialty. Mary Pickford, known as "America's Sweetheart," played innocent young girl roles. Tom Mix and his trained horse, Tony, played in western movies. Rudolf Valentino became the leading romantic male star. Charlie Chaplin was the most famous

▲ *A publicity still from* The Black Pirate, *one of the early Hollywood Technicolor movies.*

▼ *In the 1933 movie* King Kong, *a full-scale model of Kong's head and shoulders was built for certain scenes. Also constructed was a wire-operated paw.*

MOTION PICTURE

Year	Best Picture	Best Actor	Best Actress	Best Director
1927–28	*Wings*	Emil Jannings (*The Way of All Flesh* and *The Last Command*)	Janet Gaynor (*Seventh Heaven; Street Angel;* and *Sunrise*)	Frank Borzage (*Seventh Heaven*), Lewis Milestone (*Two Arabian Nights*)
1928–29	*The Broadway Melody*	Warner Baxter (*In Old Arizona*)	Mary Pickford (*Coquette*)	Frank Lloyd (*The Divine Lady*)
1929–30	*All Quiet on the Western Front*	George Arliss (*Disraeli*)	Norma Shearer (*The Divorcee*)	Lewis Milestone (*All Quiet on the Western Front*)
1930–31	*Cimarron*	Lionel Barrymore (*A Free Soul*)	Marie Dressler (*Min and Bill*)	Norman Taurog (*Skippy*)
1931–32	*Grand Hotel*	Frederic March (*Dr. Jekyll and Mr. Hyde*), Wallace Beery (*The Champ*)	Helen Hayes (*The Sin of Madelon Claudet*)	Frank Borzage (*Bad Girl*)
1932–33	*Cavalcade*	Charles Laughton (*The Private Life of Henry VIII*)	Katharine Hepburn (*Morning Glory*)	Frank Lloyd (*Cavalcade*)
1934	*It Happened One Night*	Clark Gable (*It Happened One Night*)	Claudette Colbert (*It Happened One Night*)	Frank Capra (*It Happened One Night*)
1935	*Mutiny on the Bounty*	Victor McLaglen (*The Informer*)	Bette Davis (*Dangerous*)	John Ford (*The Informer*)
1936	*The Great Ziegfeld*	Paul Muni (*The Story of Louis Pasteur*)	Luise Rainer (*The Great Ziegfeld*)	Frank Capra (*Mr. Deeds Goes to Town*)
1937	*The Life of Emile Zola*	Spencer Tracy (*Captains Courageous*)	Luise Rainer (*The Good Earth*)	Leo McCarey (*The Awful Truth*)
1938	*You Can't Take It With You*	Spencer Tracy (*Boys' Town*)	Bette Davis (*Jezebel*)	Frank Capra (*You Can't Take It With You*)
1939	*Gone With the Wind*	Robert Donat (*Goodbye Mr. Chips*)	Vivien Leigh (*Gone With the Wind*)	Victor Fleming (*Gone With the Wind*)
1940	*Rebecca*	James Stewart (*The Philadelphia Story*)	Ginger Rogers (*Kitty Foyle*)	John Ford (*The Grapes of Wrath*)
1941	*How Green Was My Valley*	Gary Cooper (*Sergeant York*)	Joan Fontaine (*Suspicion*)	John Ford (*How Green Was My Valley*)
1942	*Mrs. Miniver*	James Cagney (*Yankee Doodle Dandy*)	Greer Garson (*Mrs. Miniver*)	William Wyler (*Mrs. Miniver*)
1943	*Casablanca*	Paul Lukas (*Watch on the Rhine*)	Jennifer Jones (*The Song of Bernadette*)	Michael Curtiz (*Casablanca*)
1944	*Going My Way*	Bing Crosby (*Going My Way*)	Ingrid Bergman (*Gaslight*)	Leo McCarey (*Going My Way*)
1945	*The Lost Weekend*	Ray Milland (*The Lost Weekend*)	Joan Crawford (*Mildred Pierce*)	Billy Wilder (*The Lost Weekend*)
1946	*The Best Years of Our Lives*	Frederic March (*The Best Years of Our Lives*)	Olivia de Havilland (*To Each His Own*)	William Wyler (*The Best Years of Our Lives*)
1947	*Gentleman's Agreement*	Ronald Colman (*A Double Life*)	Loretta Young (*The Farmer's Daughter*)	Elia Kazan (*Gentleman's Agreement*)
1948	*Hamlet*	Laurence Olivier (*Hamlet*)	Jane Wyman (*Johnny Belinda*)	John Huston (*Treasure of the Sierra Madre*)
1949	*All the King's Men*	Broderick Crawford (*All the King's Men*)	Olivia de Havilland (*The Heiress*)	Joseph L. Mankievicz (*A Letter to Three Wives*)
1950	*All About Eve*	José Ferrer (*Cyrano de Bergerac*)	Judy Holliday (*Born Yesterday*)	Joseph L. Mankievicz (*All About Eve*)
1951	*An American in Paris*	Humphrey Bogart (*The African Queen*)	Vivien Leigh (*A Streetcar Named Desire*)	George Stevens (*A Place in the Sun*)
1952	*The Greatest Show on Earth*	Gary Cooper (*High Noon*)	Shirley Booth (*Come Back, Little Sheba*)	John Ford (*The Quiet Man*)
1953	*From Here to Eternity*	William Holden (*Stalag 17*)	Audrey Hepburn (*Roman Holiday*)	Fred Zinnemann (*From Here to Eternity*)
1954	*On the Waterfront*	Marlon Brando (*On the Waterfront*)	Grace Kelly (*The Country Girl*)	Elia Kazan (*On the Waterfront*)
1955	*Marty*	Ernest Borgnine (*Marty*)	Anna Magnani (*The Rose Tattoo*)	Delbert Mann (*Marty*)
1956	*Around the World in 80 Days*	Yul Brynner (*The King and I*)	Ingrid Bergman (*Anastasia*)	George Stevens (*Giant*)
1957	*The Bridge on the River Kwai*	Alec Guinness (*The Bridge on the River Kwai*)	Joanne Woodward (*The Three Faces of Eve*)	David Lean (*The Bridge on the River Kwai*)
1958	*Gigi*	David Niven (*Separate Tables*)	Susan Hayward (*I Want to Live*)	Vincente Minelli (*Gigi*)
1959	*Ben-Hur*	Charlton Heston (*Ben-Hur*)	Simone Signoret (*Room at the Top*)	William Wyler (*Ben-Hur*)

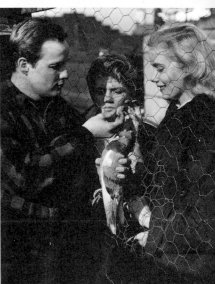

▲ *Marlon Brando in* On the Waterfront, *one of his early starring roles.*

▶ *Clark Gable and Vivien Leigh in* Gone With the Wind, *the 1939 blockbuster.*

AWARDS

◄ *Robert Redford and Meryl Streep in a scene from* Out of Africa.

▼ *Humphrey Bogart and Ingrid Bergman in the 1943 Oscar-winning film* Casablanca. *It won best film and best director (Michael Curtiz).*

Year	Best Picture	Best Actor	Best Actress	Best Director
1960	*The Apartment*	Burt Lancaster (*Elmer Gantry*)	Elizabeth Taylor (*Butterfield 8*)	Billy Wilder (*The Apartment*)
1961	*West Side Story*	Maximilian Schell (*Judgment at Nuremberg*)	Sophia Loren (*Two Women*)	Robert Wise & Jerome Robbins (*West Side Story*)
1962	*Lawrence of Arabia*	Gregory Peck (*To Kill a Mockingbird*)	Anne Bancroft (*The Miracle Worker*)	David Lean (*Lawrence of Arabia*)
1963	*Tom Jones*	Sidney Poitier (*Lilies of the Field*)	Patricia Neal (*Hud*)	Tony Richardson (*Tom Jones*)
1964	*My Fair Lady*	Rex Harrison (*My Fair Lady*)	Julie Andrews (*Mary Poppins*)	George Cukor (*My Fair Lady*)
1965	*The Sound of Music*	Lee Marvin (*Cat Ballou*)	Julie Christie (*Darling*)	Robert Wise (*The Sound of Music*)
1966	*A Man for All Seasons*	Paul Schofield (*A Man for All Seasons*)	Elizabeth Taylor (*Who's Afraid of Virginia Wolf?*)	Fred Zinnemann (*A Man for All Seasons*)
1967	*In the Heat of the Night*	Rod Steiger (*In the Heat of the Night*)	Katharine Hepburn (*Guess Who's Coming to Dinner?*)	Mike Nichols (*The Graduate*)
1968	*Oliver*	Cliff Robertson (*Charly*)	Katharine Hepburn (*A Lion in Winter*), Barbara Streisand (*Funny Girl*)	Sir Carol Reed (*Oliver*)
1969	*Midnight Cowboy*	John Wayne (*True Grit*)	Maggie Smith (*The Prime of Miss Jean Brodie*)	John Schlesinger (*Midnight Cowboy*)
1970	*Patton*	Goerge C. Scott (*Patton*)	Glenda Jackson (*Women in Love*)	Franklin J. Schaffner (*Patton*)
1971	*The French Connection*	Gene Hackman (*The French Connection*)	Jane Fonda (*Klute*)	William Friedkin (*The French Connection*)
1972	*The Godfather*	Marlon Brando (*The Godfather*)	Liza Minnelli (*Cabaret*)	Robert Fosse (*Cabaret*)
1973	*The Sting*	Jack Lemmon (*Save the Tiger*)	Glenda Jackson (*A Touch of Class*)	George Roy Hill (*The Sting*)
1974	*The Godfather Part II*	Art Carney (*Harry and Tonto*)	Ellen Burstyn (*Alice Doesn't Live Here Any More*)	Francis Ford Coppola (*The Godfather Part II*)
1975	*One Flew Over the Cuckoo's Nest*	Jack Nicholson (*One Flew Over the Cuckoo's Nest*)	Louise Fletcher (*One Flew Over the Cuckoo's Nest*)	Milos Forman (*One Flew Over the Cuckoo's Nest*)
1976	*Rocky*	Peter Finch (*Network*)	Fay Dunaway (*Network*)	John G. Avildsen (*Rocky*)
1977	*Annie Hall*	Richard Dreyfus (*Goodbye Girl*)	Diane Keaton (*Annie Hall*)	Woody Allen (*Annie Hall*)
1978	*The Deerhunter*	John Voight (*Coming Home*)	Jane Fonda (*Coming Home*)	Michael Cimino (*The Deerhunter*)
1979	*Kramer versus Kramer*	Dustin Hoffman (*Kramer versus Kramer*)	Sally Field (*Norma Rae*)	Robert Benton (*Kramer versus Kramer*)
1980	*Ordinary People*	Robert De Niro (*Raging Bull*)	Sissy Spacek (*Coalminer's Daughter*)	Robert Redford (*Ordinary People*)
1981	*Chariots of Fire*	Henry Fonda (*On Golden Pond*)	Katharine Hepburn (*On Golden Pond*)	Warren Beatty (*Reds*)
1982	*Gandhi*	Ben Kingsley (*Gandhi*)	Meryl Streep (*Sophie's Choice*)	Sir Richard Attenborough (*Gandhi*)
1983	*Terms of Endearment*	Robert Duvall (*Tender Mercies*)	Shirley MacLaine (*Terms of Endearment*)	James L. Brooks (*Terms of Endearment*)
1984	*Amadeus*	F. Murray Abraham (*Amadeus*)	Sally Field (*Places in the Heart*)	Milos Forman (*Amadeus*)
1985	*Out of Africa*	William Hurt (*Kiss of the Spider Woman*)	Geraldine Page (*The Trip to Bountiful*)	Sydney Pollack (*Out of Africa*)
1986	*Platoon*	Paul Newman (*The Color of Money*)	Marlee Martin (*Children of a Lesser God*)	Oliver Stone (*Platoon*)
1987	*The Last Emperor*	Michael Douglas (*Wall Street*)	Cher (*Moonstruck*)	Bernardo Bertolucci (*The Last Emperor*)
1988	*Rain Main*	Dustin Hoffman (*Rain Main*)	Jodie Foster (*The Accused*)	Barry Levinson (*Rain Man*)
1989	*Driving Miss Daisy*	Daniel Day-Lewis (*My Left Foot*)	Jessica Tandy (*Driving Miss Daisy*)	Oliver Stone (*Born on the Fourth of July*)
1990	*Dances with Wolves*	Jeremy Irons (*Reversal of Fortune*)	Kathy Bates (*Misery*)	Kevin Costner (*Dances with Wolves*)

▲ *Rudolf Valentino*

▲ *Humphrey Bogart*

▲ *John Wayne*

▲ *Christopher Reeve*

comedian. He played a sad, but always hopeful, tramp. Movies called *serials* became very popular. These were movies made in short chapters. One chapter was shown at a time. Each one ended with the hero in desperate danger, perhaps hanging from a cliff, so that the audience would be sure to come back the following week to see what happened. Serials were sometimes called *cliffhangers*. The *Perils of Pauline* was a favorite.

European Film Making Moviemaking began in Europe at about the same time as in the United States. But during World War I, European film makers had to stop production. Hollywood movies became international favorites. After the war, Europeans again began to make their own motion pictures.

The Germans began to make films that explored the human mind. *The Cabinet of Doctor Caligari*, directed by Robert Weine in 1919, was one of these. It was photographed as if seen through the eyes of a person in a mental institution. The Germans also contributed many new technical advances to film making. The French began to make films that were truly individual in style. These films often were intimate studies of lower-class life in France. Film making in the Soviet Union came under government control. Soviet directors, among them Sergei Eisenstein, began to use the film to teach their audiences about Communist ideals. European moviemaking was again interrupted by World War II. But the trend toward making more realistic movies continued after the war.

▶ *Horror movies, such as those featuring the infamous Count Dracula, often demand all the skills of the make-up artist and the special effects department.*

When films made in one country are shown in a country speaking a different language, something has to be done to the films so that the viewers will understand them. For instance, for a film in which French is spoken, a new sound track is made with English-speaking actors speaking the words. This process is called *dubbing*. Another way of making a foreign film understandable is to print at the bottom of the picture an English translation of the words spoken by the actors. The printed words are called *subtitles*.

The Beginning of Sound When radio programs became popular about 1925, many people stopped attending movies. But in 1927, the first sound film, *The Jazz Singer*, starring Al Jolson, was put out by Warner Brothers. It had only a few lines of dialogue and several songs, but it was an immediate success. The new "talkies" replaced the silent films. Many actors and actresses with foreign accents or unpleasant-sounding voices lost their jobs. Comedians, such as the rowdy Marx Brothers and W. C. Fields,

▲ *Mattresses break the fall for this group of Mexican stuntmen. Stuntmen are the unseen "stars" of many action films.*

introduced a new type of film humor. Lively movies, called *musicals,* filled with dancing and singing, were made. Fred Astaire and Ginger Rogers were dancing partners in a long list of happy musicals. Shirley Temple, with her dimples and golden curls, became one of the world's best-loved child actresses. Gangster, detective, and horror stories were filmed too.

In 1933, a way of filming movies in color was perfected. It was called *Technicolor.* One of the biggest and most successful of Technicolor films was *Gone With the Wind,* a Civil War drama shot in 1939. The new color process made the film's elaborate costumes and sets seem more real. *Gone With the Wind* is considered a milestone in film making.

Cartoons, or *animated* films, began to use both sound and color. Cartoons are made by showing a series of drawings one after another so that the drawn pictures seem to move. Walt Disney, a famous American cartoonist, began by making short, silent black-and-white cartoons. His make-believe stars, Mickey Mouse and Donald Duck, became as popular as real actors. Disney made the first full-length color cartoon, *Snow White and the Seven Dwarfs,* in 1937.

Documentaries Beginning in the 1920's, some moviemakers became interested in using movies to record events in real life. These were called *documentaries.* An American named Robert Flaherty made the first important documentary, *Nanook of the North,* in 1922. It showed the hardships of Eskimo life and the beauty of the isolated Arctic. John Grierson made the first British documentary, *Drifters,* in 1929. It was about a fishing fleet at sea. Documentaries became an important device for spreading information during World War II.

Challenge to American Motion Picture Making Just as radio took away early silent movie customers, television also had its effect on motion picture audiences. Some people began to stay home and watch movies on television. Others began to prefer the simpler, more realistic movies being made by European film makers. Hollywood moviemakers tried to fight back by using sensational techniques in movies. They developed Cinemascope and Cinerama with a larger screen and stereophonic sound, which made the audience feel as if the movie was going on all around them. *The Robe,* a Biblical story, was shown in 1953. *Around the World in 80 Days, South Pacific,* and *The Sound of Music,* followed. Dazzling new color techniques and 3-D (3-dimensional) movies were also perfected. The 3-D movies made it seem as if images could jump right out of the screen into the audience. But viewers had to wear special glasses to watch the movies, and 3-D never really caught on.

▲ *Bette Davis*

▲ *Ingrid Bergman*

▲ *Marilyn Monroe*

▲ *Meryl Streep*

1663

▲ *Modern spectacular films often make use of specially designed sets and equipment costing large sums of money. The realistic looking spaceship shown here was built for use in the highly successful movie* Star Wars. *Many special effects for the film were created with the use of a computer.*

2001, A Space Odyssey, was an experimental Cinerama (wraparound screen) movie. Viewers felt they were on a journey through space. Experimental techniques with light were used in this picture. The big Hollywood companies began to sell their movies to television and to make special films just for television. Some of the Hollywood producers went out of business. Others began to imitate the realism in European films and make less expensive motion pictures.

Movies Today and Tomorrow
Today motion pictures face a new threat from home video cassette recorders (VCR's). For a small cost, people can now watch feature films in the comfort of their own homes, and fewer go to movie theaters regularly. Modern movies depend more on good stories and filming techniques than on glamorous stars and elaborate sets. They are created for more than just amusement. Motion pictures help teach subjects in schools and colleges. The armed forces use educational films to train soldiers, too. Business executives use movies to train employees and to tell their customers about their products. Many high schools and colleges offer courses in film making. Even elementary school classes make films now.

Movies are not even 100 years old. But the British art historian Kenneth Clark predicted that people living 100 years from now will look back on film making as the greatest art form of our century.

ALSO READ: ACTORS AND ACTING; CAMERA; CARTOONING; DISNEY, WALT; DRAMA; MAKEUP; MUSICAL COMEDY; PHOTOGRAPHY; TELEVISION; THEATER.

MOTOR A motor can be defined as a device that changes any form of energy into mechanical energy or motion. An engine is a kind of motor that consumes fuel in converting energy into mechanical power, as in an automobile or truck. An *electric motor* is an arrangement of magnets and wire coils that changes a special kind of energy—electric current—into mechanical power or motion. Electric motors are used every day in all kinds of electrical equipment found in most homes. Refrigerators, vacuum cleaners, sewing machines, record players, irons, washing machines, and fans are run by motors.

The action of magnetism is the principle on which an electric motor is based. The relationship between electricity and magnetism was discovered in 1819, when Hans Christian Oersted found that a wire carrying an electric current has a magnetic field around it. In other words, he discovered that electricity and magnetism are related. Shortly after this, other scientists discovered that a piece of iron becomes a magnet when it is put inside a coil of wire carrying electric current. They also found that the coil and iron together, called an *electromagnet*, had even greater magnetism. The British scientist Michael Faraday first had the idea of putting this electromagnetism to work in the form of a motor.

Even today, the principle on which an electric motor operates is similar to

Faraday's idea. Mechanical power or motion is produced because of the attraction of *unlike* magnetic fields for each other and the repulsion of *like* magnetic fields from each other. In the simplest motor, a loop or coil of wire is attached to a metal stick, or *shaft*. The shaft is then suspended between the two poles of a permanent magnet.

When electric current is sent through the wire (perhaps from a battery), the unlike magnetic fields on the permanent magnet and electromagnet pull toward each other, and the like magnetic fields push away from each other. This causes the shaft and the wire to move in some direction—forward, up, down—depending on the location of the poles of the permanent magnet. When the electric current going through the wire is reversed, or sent in the opposite direction, the magnetic fields in the electromagnet are also reversed. This causes the shaft to move again—in the opposite direction. A steady movement of the motor is produced by a

▶ *A simple electric motor operates on the principles of magnetism— that is, unlike magnetic fields attract each other and like magnetic fields repel each other. To make use of this principle, a loop or coil of wire is attached to a metal shaft and suspended between the poles of a permanent magnet: (1) The magnetic fields interact, and forces of attraction and repulsion cause the coil to turn. (2) The poles of the coil are almost in line with the poles of the permanent magnets, and the carbon brushes are almost at the ends of the commutator segments. (3) The coil cannot stop when its poles are aligned with those of the permanent magnet. The momentum of the coil carries it past this point. At the same time, the commutator reverses the current flowing through the coil, thus reversing the magnetic poles of the coil. (4) Forces of attraction and repulsion keep the coil turning. (5) The poles of the coil again pass those of the magnet, the current through the coil reverses, and the coil keeps turning around.*

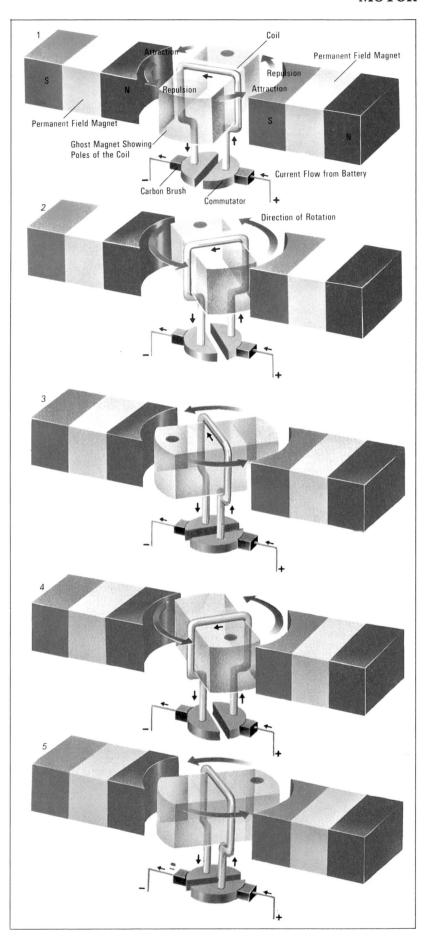

▲ *The badge of the Scott Motorcycle Company, one of the early manufacturers still in existence today.*

pair of metal strips, or *brushes*, connected to the battery or other power source. The brushes alternately touch the wire as it rotates on the shaft and provide a regular "feeding" of electric current. The regular reversal of the direction of the current keeps the shaft—and the electromagnet—moving. This movement is the power that is generated by a motor to operate a machine.

The more electric current given to a motor, the more power the motor generates. An electric fan motor, for example, produces more mechanical power than the motor in an electric clock does. Therefore, a fan motor uses more current.

ALSO READ: ELECTRIC APPLIANCE; ELECTRICITY; ELECTROMAGNET; ENGINE; FARADAY, MICHAEL; MAGNET.

MOTORBOAT see BOATS AND BOATING.

MOTORCYCLE When gasoline and steam engines were first developed, people began trying to find a practical way of attaching a motor to a bicycle. The result, later called a motorcycle, would be faster than a bicycle and less tiring to operate. In 1885, Gottlieb Daimler, a German inventor, attached a gasoline engine to a bicycle. His invention was the model for early motorcycles.

Today, however, motorcycles do not look nearly so much like bicycles. They are much wider and heavier than bikes. A motorcycle has an *engine*, which is mounted between the two wheels, with a *gas tank* above it. The driver sits astride the cycle on a padded *saddle*, or seat. Front and rear *springs* make the ride fairly comfortable for the motorcyclist.

▼ *The "Flying Finn" Heikki Mikkola takes off during a motocross race.*

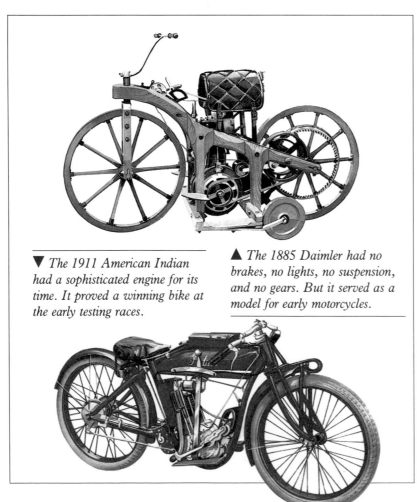

▼ *The 1911 American Indian had a sophisticated engine for its time. It proved a winning bike at the early testing races.*

▲ *The 1885 Daimler had no brakes, no lights, no suspension, and no gears. But it served as a model for early motorcycles.*

The driver starts the motorcycle with the *starter button* on the handlebars or the *starter crank pedal* below the seat (operated with the foot). He or she shifts gears by pressing the *clutch hand lever* on the left handlebar and the *gear shift* (below the engine) with the left foot. The driver stops the motorcycle by using the *front brake hand lever* on the right handlebar and the *rear brake foot pedal* beside the motorcycle engine.

There are various kinds of motorcycles. A *touring bike* weighs several hundred pounds, can carry heavy loads, and can go at a high speed. It is often used for cross-country travel. A *trail bike* is not as heavy and fast as a touring bike. It is used on rugged country trails and roads and for climbing steep hills. A *motor scooter* is smaller than an ordinary motorcycle, and the driver's feet rest on a floorboard, not astride a saddle as in a motorcycle. There are also *minicycles*

(compact, sturdy motorcycles), *minibikes* (lightweight bikes with motorcycle-type engines), and *mopeds* (small, motorized bicycles).

Many cyclists compete in annual events (such as a motocross rally) held in the United States, Canada, and other countries. Most of the U. S. events are governed by the American Motorcycle Association (AMA).

Motorcycles are a popular form of transportation. They are more fuel-efficient and cheaper to buy and operate than cars, and they are faster than bicycles. They can be dangerous, however, and it is important for cyclists to wear proper safety equipment and observe the rules of safe "biking" at all times. The police often use motorcycles, especially three-wheeled ones, because their small size permits them to move easily through traffic.

ALSO READ: BICYCLE, ENGINE, GEAR, MOTOR.

▲ *Honda's VFR750F is based on a powerful V-4 750cc engine, which develops 105 horsepower.*

▼ *One type of motorcycle race is speedway. Speedway has its own special techniques, machines, and clothing. Riders rely on a skillful combination of speed and balance.*

◀ *The British rider Joey Dunlop won the Isle of Man TT race in 1980 and again in 1985.*

▼ *Two BMW bikes—one of the K100 range and the 3-cylinder K75.*

MOUNTAIN

Strange as it seems, the rock in the world's highest mountain chain, the Himalayas, began at the bottom of a great sea. Over millions of years the rock has been lifted and folded into mountains such as Everest.

MOUNTAIN All over the Earth the giant rigid plates that form the Earth's crust are slowly moving. When they collide, the rocks in between are squeezed until they buckle, forming mountains. These are called *fold* mountains, and they form the highest and most extensive mountain ranges in the world. The Appalachian Mountains are an example of fold mountains. The lowland between mountains is called a *valley*, through which streams or rivers flow.

Block mountains are formed when huge masses of rock move up or down along cracks, or *faults*, in the Earth's surface. Steep cliffs result from this type of Earth movement. The Sierra Nevada Mountains in California are an example of block mountains. Earthquakes are also caused by these Earth shifts.

Another way a mountain can be born is through *volcanic action*. Molten rock deep in the Earth forces its way up to the surface. On February 20, 1943, an extraordinary eruption occurred in a cornfield in west central Mexico. A new volcano, Parícutin, pushed up through the Earth's crust. Showers of hot rocks and lava burst through an opening in the earth. The cinder cone formed by their ashes was 100 feet (30 m) high by the second day. It was 450 feet (137 m) high two weeks later. When it stopped erupting in 1952, the cone of Parícutin was about 2,000 feet (610 m) high. Vol-

The zones on a tropical mountain form distinct bands at different altitudes. Tropical vegetation at the foot gives way to deciduous forest at about 3,000 feet (900 m). This, in turn, gives way to coniferous forest, which is succeeded by a zone of shrubby plants. They eventually give way to grassland and a zone of sparse lichens and sedges just below the snow line.

▼ *Different kinds of fold mountains. A* nappe *is a fold pushed forward over the rocks. A fold may be tilted over to form a* recumbent *fold. Below, opposite page, shows how block mountains are thrown up. The blocks of land pushed upward are called* horsts; *the steep slopes bordering horsts are called* fault scarps.

| Nappe | Recumbent fold | Anticline | Syncline | Anticlinorium |

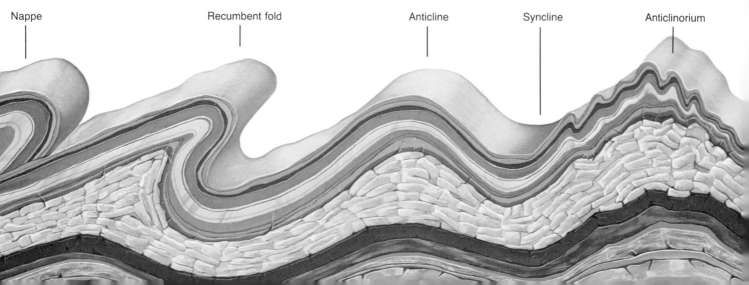

Snow line

Timber line

◀ *The Himalayas, the world's highest fold mountains, were pushed up where the Indian subcontinent met the continent of Asia.*

canic action can also push the earth up into *dome* mountains. These high, rounded mountains are like blisters full of hot liquid when they are first formed. But the liquid later cools and forms solid rock. Elk Mountain in Wyoming is a dome mountain.

No sooner is a mountain formed than *erosion* sets in. Wind, rain, frost, and snow slowly wear away the rock and produce an endless variety of mountain shapes. The highest mountain on land is Mount Everest— 29,028 feet (8,848 m) high. But the Earth's greatest mountains lie beneath the sea. They are higher and more rugged than those on land because they are not worn down by erosion. The tips of some undersea mountains form islands in the middle of the ocean. Mauna Loa, the famous volcano on the island of Hawaii, is the tip of an undersea mountain. Measured from the ocean floor, Mauna Loa is nearly 1,000 feet (305 m) higher than Mount Everest.

Plants that only grow high up on mountains are called *alpine* plants. Trees will usually not survive any higher than about 11,000 feet (3,350 m). The point where alpine shrubs, mosses, and bare rock replace trees is called the *timberline*. A number of animals can live in the wind, cold,

Where is the highest known mountain? Strangely enough, it is not Mount Everest and it is not on Earth. It is Olympus Mons (Mount Olympus) on Mars, and is 95,000 feet (29,000 m) high—over three times as high as Mount Everest.

The higher you go up a mountain, the colder it gets. The temperature drops by 3°F for every 1,000 feet (5°C for every 300 m) you go up.

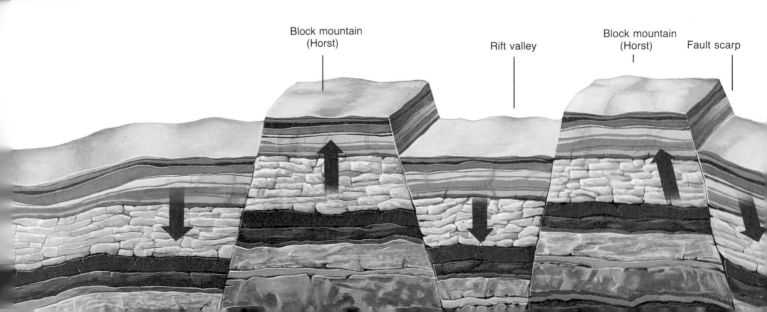

Block mountain (Horst)

Rift valley

Block mountain (Horst)

Fault scarp

INTERESTING MOUNTAINS IN THE SEVEN CONTINENTS OF THE WORLD

	Name	Height (in feet)	Height (in meters)	Location	
AFRICA	Kilimanjaro—(has 2 peaks)				Highest mountain in Africa
	Kibo	19,340	5,895	Tanzania	
	Mawenzi	17,564	5,354	Tanzania	
ANTARCTICA	Vinson Massif	16,860	5,139	Chilean sector	Highest mountain in Antarctica
ASIA	Everest	29,028	8,848	Nepal-Tibet border	Highest mountain in Asia and the world
	Fuji	12,389	3,776	Japan	Sacred mountain to many Japanese
	Nebo	2,625	800	Jordan	Peak from which Moses looked out at the Promised Land
AUSTRALIA	Kosciusko	7,316	2,230	New South Wales	Highest mountain in Australia
EUROPE	Elbrus	18,481	5,633	Soviet Union	Highest mountain in Europe
	Matterhorn	14,780	4,505	Switzerland-Italy border	Skilled mountain climbers scale its peak
	Mount Etna	10,902	3,323	Italy	} Active volcanoes in Europe
	Vesuvius	4,200	1,280	Italy	
NORTH AMERICA	McKinley	20,320	6,194	Alaska	Highest mountain in North America
	Pikes Peak	14,110	4,301	Colorado	First peak of the Rockies that can be seen by people coming from the east
	Lassen Peak	10,446	3,190	California	} Active volcanoes in the contiguous United States
	St. Helens	9,677	2,950	Washington	
SOUTH AMERICA	Aconcagua	22,834	6,960	Argentina	Highest mountain in South America
	Cotopaxi	19,347	5,897	Ecuador	Highest active volcano in the world

▼ *Mount Fuji, Japan's highest mountain, is a volcano which was last active in 1707. It reaches a height of 12,355 feet (3,766 m) above sea level.*

poor vegetation, and thin air of the mountains. Some of the best-known mountain animals in North America are the bighorn sheep, Rocky Mountain goat, marmot, snowshoe rabbit, and mountain lion. People, too, can live at high altitudes. Mountain climbers from the lowlands often bring an oxygen supply with them. But the Indians of the Andes and the mountain people of the Himalayas are used to the thin air. They need no extra oxygen.

Mountains have long played an important part throughout history in deciding boundaries between countries. The Pyrenees separate France from Spain. The Himalayas provide a high barrier between India and China. Mountains have checked conquering armies and often forced them to retreat. A gap through a mountain chain can often prove important in history. The Cumberland Gap in the Appalachian Mountains provided a passageway to the West for thousands of American pioneers.

ALSO READ: ALPS MOUNTAINS, ANDES MOUNTAINS, APPALACHIAN MOUNTAINS, ATMOSPHERE, AVALANCHE, CANYON, CAUCASUS MOUNTAINS, EARTHQUAKE, EROSION, GEOLOGY, HIMALAYA MOUNTAINS, MOUNTAIN CLIMBING, ROCKY MOUNTAINS, URAL MOUNTAINS, VOLCANO.

MOUNTAIN CLIMBING Mountain climbing is a sport in which men and women climb the slopes of hills and mountains on foot. Mountaineers (climbers) must be in excellent physical condition and must be experienced in climbing techniques in order to survive. Some people enjoy climbing relatively gentle slopes as a hobby. But a few people are willing to risk their lives in order to conquer the highest mountain peaks in the world.

▼ *Mountain climbers check their ropes on the rugged cliffs and jagged peaks of the Dolomites, which are part of the Alps, a folded mountain system.*

In Great Britain, the craggy hills of Wales and Scotland are popular with mountaineers. The high peaks of the Alps in Europe attract climbers from many countries. The Andes Mountains in South America and the Himalayas in Asia also offer challenges to mountain climbers. The Rockies in the western United States have many peaks that attract mountaineering fans.

Mountain climbing clubs have been established for people interested in the sport. The oldest, England's Alpine Club, was established in 1858. Clubs in this country include the American Alpine Club, the Sierra Club, and the Appalachian Mountain Club. These and similar organizations train climbers and interested beginners in the best and safest methods of climbing.

Many special kinds of equipment are used in mountain climbing. Climbers wear heavy boots with cleated soles to prevent slipping on steep inclines. To climb on ice, mountaineers attach *crampons*, frames with special steel spikes, to their boots. When climbers travel over steep rocks and icy slopes, they are often tied to each other with long ropes. Then one person at a time moves forward. If someone slips, the others, who are tied to that person, can prevent him or her from falling too far. Iron spikes called *pitons* may be driven into the rock to provide footholds or places to attach ropes. Climbers carry ice axes to cut footholds in ice. Ice axes are also used as walking sticks on difficult slopes. Climbers wear dark glasses to protect their eyes from the blinding snow, and insulated clothing, to keep themselves warm. Climbers wear backpacks containing first aid and cooking equipment and food. If the climb is to take more than one day, they must carry tents and sleeping bags in their backpacks. If the peak is very high, where the air has little oxygen, climbers bring tanks of oxygen with them.

▲ *Mountaineers Sir Edmund Hillary with Sherpa Tenzing Norgay. They were the first men to scale the summit of Mount Everest, the world's highest mountain. They achieved this on May 29, 1953, standing at the summit for 15 minutes.*

Mountain climbing first became popular in Europe in the 1800's. Expeditions of mountaineers began climbing the highest and most difficult peaks in the world during the 1900's. In 1953, the summit of Mount Everest, the world's highest mountain, was reached by Sir Edmund Hillary and Tenzing Norkay. Some of the world's highest peaks still remain to be conquered.

ALSO READ: HILLARY, SIR EDMUND; HIMALAYA MOUNTAINS; MOUNTAIN.

MOUNT VERNON see WASHINGTON, GEORGE.

MOVIE see MOTION PICTURE.

MOZAMBIQUE Mozambique, formerly called Portuguese East Africa, is bounded by Tanzania on the north, Malawi and Zambia on the northwest, and Zimbabwe on the west and southwest. The east coast stretches along the Indian Ocean for 1,736 miles (2,794 km). (See the map with the article on AFRICA.)

▼ *Fishing is important in Mozambique, which has a larger coastal plain than other East African nations.*

Mozambique's ports are important for the importing of goods to the African interior and for exporting of goods to the rest of the world. Maputo, the capital and largest city, is an important seaport. Beira is the other leading seaport.

There are lowlands along the coast of Mozambique and high, grassy open plains, called *savannas*, in the interior. Mozambique is a hot, tropical country with seasonal rainy and dry periods. Farming is the most important industry. Sugarcane, corn, cotton, coconuts, tea, and other crops are grown, usually on large plantations. It is the world's leading producer of cashew nuts. Mozambique has rich mineral deposits, which have been only partially mined.

In 1498, Vasco da Gama, a Portuguese navigator, was the first European to explore the coastal area of Mozambique. The Portuguese founded settlements along the coast during the 1500's, and Mozambique was a colony of Portugal for 470 years. Slavery was commonplace in Mozambique from the late 1500's until the present century. Slaves captured in the interior were often shipped out and sold in other parts of the world, especially Brazil, until the middle 1800's. Slavery was completely abolished in Mozambique after 1928.

Most of the people of Mozambique are black Africans who speak one of several Bantu languages. There are also some Portuguese and Asians.

From 1964 until 1974, the Front for the Liberation of Mozambique (Frelimo) waged a guerilla war against Portuguese colonial rule. In 1975, Mozambique became an independent nation. Its government was led by President Samora Machel until he died in a plane crash in 1986. Machel was succeeded as president by Joaquim Chissano. Since independence, Mozambique has had a Socialist government allied to the U.S.S.R. It has suffered droughts and a civil

MOZAMBIQUE

Capital City: Maputo (884,000 people).

Area: 302,330 square miles (782,974 sq. km).

Population: 14,800,000.

Government: People's republic.

Natural Resources: Coal, iron, ore, diamonds, gold, natural gas, titanium.

Export Products: Shrimps, cashew nuts, sugar, copra, citrus fruit.

Unit of Money: Metical.

Official Language: Portuguese.

war, with government troops fighting a right-wing guerrilla force, the Mozambique National Resistance.

ALSO READ: AFRICA, PORTUGAL, SLAVERY.

MOZART, WOLFGANG AMADEUS (1756–1791)

The great composer, Wolfgang Amadeus Mozart, began to write music when he was five years old. He was giving public concerts of his own music at the age of six. Although Mozart had a short and tragic life, his works have remained among the world's greatest classical musical compositions.

Mozart was born in Salzburg, Austria. His father, Leopold Mozart, was a composer and violinist. He gave Wolfgang and his elder sister, Maria Anna, musical training and took them on concert tours throughout Europe. The two children gave many public performances on the harpsichord (an early type of piano) and even played for kings and queens. Everyone liked the happy, lively boy and was amazed at his talents. Wolfgang never went to school but he learned about different musical styles from the musicians he met in his travels.

At the age of 14, Mozart became concertmaster at the court of the archbishop of Salzburg. The young musician was poorly paid there, and he was constantly trying to find a better job. He finally left the archbishop in 1781 and went to live in Vienna. He married and tried to support his family by giving music lessons and by working day and night at his compositions, but he became very poor. In 1787, Mozart was appointed court composer to the Austrian emperor.

A mysterious stranger asked Mozart to compose a Requiem mass (music for a funeral service) in 1791. Mozart was very ill at the time. He is said to have thought about his own funeral while composing the *Requiem*, which was unfinished when he died (probably from hard, incessant work). A pupil later completed it.

Mozart wrote more than 600 musical compositions. His music has a lively, vigorous spirit and beautiful melodies that still sound fresh. He wrote several lovely operas, such as *The Magic Flute* and *Don Giovanni*, and many symphonies.

ALSO READ: COMPOSER.

MUHAMMAD (about A.D. 570–632)

Muhammad was the founder of Islam, one of the world's great religions. He was born in the Arabian city of Mecca, a busy trading and religious center. Muhammad's family belonged to the ruling tribe of Quraish in Mecca. His parents died when Muhammad was a baby, and he was raised by his uncle.

▲ *The young Mozart in a violet dress suit trimmed with gold braid, given to him in Vienna in 1762 by the Empress Maria-Theresa. His father, Leopold Mozart, had him painted in it as a souvenir.*

By the age of three, Mozart was playing chords on the clavichord and harpsichord. By four, he was playing minuets. At six he wrote a concerto and toured Europe's royal courts, singing and playing the piano, clavichord, and violin. If his audience paid too little attention, Mozart stopped playing and burst into tears.

▶ *Muhammad, the founder of the Islamic religion, was in his 40's when he began preaching the new religion.*

▼ *Brian Mulroney, Prime Minister of Canada.*

Muhammad became a camel driver, and later a merchant, and traveled a few times with trading caravans. He was deeply religious and spent many hours in prayer. The Arab tribes at the time worshiped many gods. But Muhammad believed in only one true God. When he was 40 years old, he began to have visions. He believed that the angel Gabriel appeared and told him to teach the words of God. His wife, Khadija, believed in his visions, and soon he had other followers, who called him the prophet of God. The words that he heard in his visions were written down and later collected in the *Koran*.

Muhammad angered the merchants of Mecca by criticizing their greedy lives. He was persecuted in Mecca and was forced to flee to Medina, a nearby city, in A.D. 622. This flight is called the *Hegira*, and the Muslim calendar dates from it. He was invited to Medina to make peace between warring tribes, and he even became governor. In A.D. 630, Muhammad returned to Mecca and captured the city. Most of the people were converted to Islam.

Muhammad died two years later, but the faith of Islam spread rapidly. Its followers, Muslims or Moslems, number about 550 million. Islam forbids images, or likenesses, so no pic-

tures or statues of Muhammad were ever made. The *Sunna*, or traditions, is a record of the sayings and deeds of Muhammad collected after his death by Muslim leaders.

ALSO READ: ISLAM, KORAN, MOSQUE.

MULE see DONKEY.

MULRONEY, BRIAN (born 1939) Canada's prime minister was born Martin Brian Mulroney on March 20, 1939, in the town of Baie Comeau in Quebec province. He grew up speaking both English and fluent French. He studied at Saint Francis Xavier University in Nova Scotia and at Laval University in Quebec City, graduating in law in 1962.

While practicing law, he served on a commission investigating organized crime in the construction industry. He joined the Progressive-Conservative Party and tried unsuccessfully to win the party leadership in 1976.

In 1983, Mulroney became party leader. Although he was not well know, he led his party to a landslide victory in the 1984 general election. As prime minister, he sought agreements with the U.S. government on defense. In 1988, Mulroney was re-elected with a decisive majority. He immediately introduced a controversial free trade agreement with the United States. In 1991, he tried to recapture his dwindling popularity with a major cabinet reshuffle. But he lost much support by introducing an unpopular package of constitutional reforms.

MULTIPLE BIRTH see REPRODUCTION.

MULTIPLICATION see ARITHMETIC, MATHEMATICS.

MUMPS see CHILDHOOD DISEASES.

MURDER Murder is the killing of a human being on purpose and without legal justification (defense). It is considered the most serious crime.

There are different kinds of murder recognized by law in the United States. *Justifiable homicide* is a killing that has legal justification, such as murder in self-defense. *Excusable homicide* is an accidental killing, such as a person walking in front of a carefully driven car and being killed. If a person is killed because of a car driver's negligence (failure to act wisely), it is called *involuntary manslaughter*. *Voluntary manslaughter* is killing a person in anger, after being provoked (aroused) by the victim.

A murderer may be sent to a state or federal prison or *penitentiary* for a long period (sometimes for the rest of his or her life) or may be put to death. The death penalty, however, has been abolished in many countries.

ALSO READ: CRIME, TRIAL.

MURRAY-DARLING RIVERS
The Great Dividing Range of mountains extends along the eastern coast of Australia. Water from rain and

▼ *Lights from the river cruiser are reflected in the smooth waters of the Murray River in Australia.*

melting snow on the western slopes of the mountains runs down into several rivers. The longest of these is the Darling River, which flows southwestward for about 1,700 miles (2,740 km). At Wentworth, Australia, the Darling joins the Murray River, which has already flowed northwestward for 1,600 miles (2,575 km) from the Australian Alps (part of the Great Dividing Range). The Murray-Darling, sometimes just called the Murray River, then travels southward to empty into the Indian Ocean, near Adelaide. The Murray River, 2,310 miles (3,715 km) long from the mountains to the ocean, is Australia's longest river. It and its tributaries drain an area larger than that of Texas, Oklahoma, and Louisiana combined. (See the map with the article on AUSTRALIA.)

Both the Darling and the Murray rivers flow very slowly. The Darling River often dries up completely in years when there is very little rain. But the Murray is the only river in Australia that can be navigated for long distances. Side-wheeled steamboats once traveled up and down the river carrying wool, grain, and other commercial products. Today, these goods are transported by trains and trucks.

Engineers have devised ways to add more water to the Murray River. Reservoirs and dams were built high in the mountains of the Great Dividing Range to catch water that would normally have run off down the eastern slopes.

ALSO READ: AUSTRALIA, RIVER.

MUSCLE Bones and various organs of the body cannot move by themselves. They are moved by muscles. The human body contains more than 600 main muscles and thousands of very small ones.

Muscles move by *contracting*. Muscle cells seem able to "bunch to-

A cramp is the continuous contraction of a muscle. This painful complaint is often caused by a lack of oxygen in the muscle, usually after violent exercise. A cramp may also be caused by poor blood circulation or by swimming in cold water too soon after a meal.

▼ *Over a hundred different face muscles helped to give the Mona Lisa her fascinating smile.*

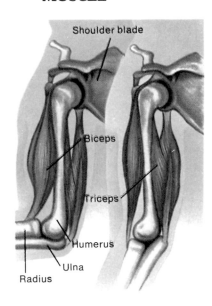

Shoulder blade

Biceps

Triceps

Humerus

Ulna

Radius

▲ *Muscles act in pairs. To bend your arm, you contract your biceps muscle (above left), and your forearm is pulled toward the upper arm. When you want to straighten your arm, your biceps muscle relaxes. At the same time, the triceps muscle contracts, pulling on the back of the Ulna bone and straightening the arm.*

It has been calculated that you use over 200 different muscles when you walk.

gether" to make the muscle shorter or more compact. Muscle contraction is caused by *myofibril*—chains of protein inside the muscle cells. These protein chains seem to be able to slide over each other and make the muscle contract.

Muscles are divided into three types—skeletal, smooth, and cardiac. Most *skeletal muscles* are attached to bones by tough white cords called *tendons*. The muscles of the face have no tendons and are attached directly to the bone. Both ends of a muscle are attached to the bone.

Skeletal muscles vary in size, depending on the work they do. The muscles that move your eyeballs are smaller and weaker than the muscles that move your legs. Skeletal muscles are of two kinds. The *flexors* bend a joint or contract inward toward the body. When you bend your elbow or make a fist, you are using flexor muscles. The *extensors* straighten a joint or pull outward away from the body. When you straighten your arm or open your fist, you are using extensors.

Skeletal muscles contain nerves. The nerves send a signal, or *stimulus*, to the muscles to make them contract. The stimulus can be a signal from the brain to the nerves. When you want to grasp a pencil, your brain sends signals to the nerves that control your finger, hand, and arm muscles. These muscles then contract, moving your hand and arm to the proper position. The stimulus can also come from outside your body. When you touch something hot, the nerves sense the heat and send a stimulus to your muscles that makes you jerk your hand away. This is called a *reflex* action. Skeletal muscles cannot contract if they are unable to receive a stimulus from the nerves. When nerves are damaged and unable to stimulate certain muscles, these muscles are *paralyzed*.

Most skeletal muscles are voluntary. "Voluntary" means that you

may consciously use your brain to control the action of the muscle. "Involuntary" means that the muscle works without your help. The diaphragm below your chest controls your breathing. It is an involuntary muscle because it can work without your thinking about it. When you take control of the diaphragm by thinking about breathing, it works as a voluntary muscle.

Smooth muscles are not attached to bones but are contained in various body organs. Smooth muscles in the stomach and intestines slowly contract and relax to move food that is being digested. Muscles in the blood vessels control blood flow.

All smooth muscles are involuntary. You cannot control them. These muscles may also work without stimuli from nerves. Their contractions are controlled by hormones. When you are angry or afraid, for example, your adrenal glands produce hormones that contract muscles in certain arteries, especially those that "feed" major internal organs. This forces more blood to your brain and skeletal muscles to make you more alert and prepare you for fighting or running.

Cardiac muscle is the muscle of the heart. It is an involuntary muscle and is the only type of muscle that can contract in a definite rhythm. Scientists do not know what causes the cardiac muscle to contract this way. They do know that the heart has a built-in pacemaker. A stimulus received from the nerves can speed up or slow down the beat but cannot control the rhythm.

Besides nerve or hormone stimulus, all muscles need energy in order to work. Energy is supplied from the food you eat. Muscle cells contain *enzymes* that constantly break down digested food and turn it into energy. Muscle cells can store energy in the form of a substance called ATP (adenosine tri-phosphate). When energy is needed, the ATP is released.

If you use your muscles for a long time, waste material collects in the muscle tissue, and your muscles lose some of their ability to contract. This is called *muscle fatigue.* Your body feels tired and needs rest in order to remove the wastes.

Muscles get bigger if they are given a great deal of use. A ballet dancer's leg muscles or a weightlifter's arm and shoulder muscles are usually larger than most people's. Muscles become smaller if they are not used. Paralyzed muscles eventually shrink to a small size.

People whose muscles contract quickly and powerfully are said to have "good muscle tone." Muscles can get "out of tone" by not having enough exercise. Muscle tone can be improved with more exercise. But too much exercise of a muscle that is not prepared for it can cause *muscle strain.* The muscle stretches or tears and soreness results. When a muscle is overworked, it may *cramp.* Cramps are strong, knotlike contractions that cause pain and may paralyze the muscle for a while. The cure is to relax the cramped muscles with heat and massage or injections given by a doctor.

ALSO READ: BONE, BRAIN, CELL, CIR-CULATORY SYSTEM, DIGESTION, EN-ERGY, ENZYME, GLAND, HEART, HU-MAN BODY, NERVOUS SYSTEM.

MUSES The myths of ancient Greece tell of nine goddesses called the Muses. They were young maidens who watched over the arts and sciences. The Muses were the daughters of Zeus, king of the gods, and Mnemosyne, goddess of memory. They often entertained the other gods and goddesses on Mount Olympus with songs and stories.

Each Muse had a special art or science of her own, symbolized in Greek art by a particular sign. Clio, the Muse of history, carried a scroll, or rolled document. Thalia, who wore

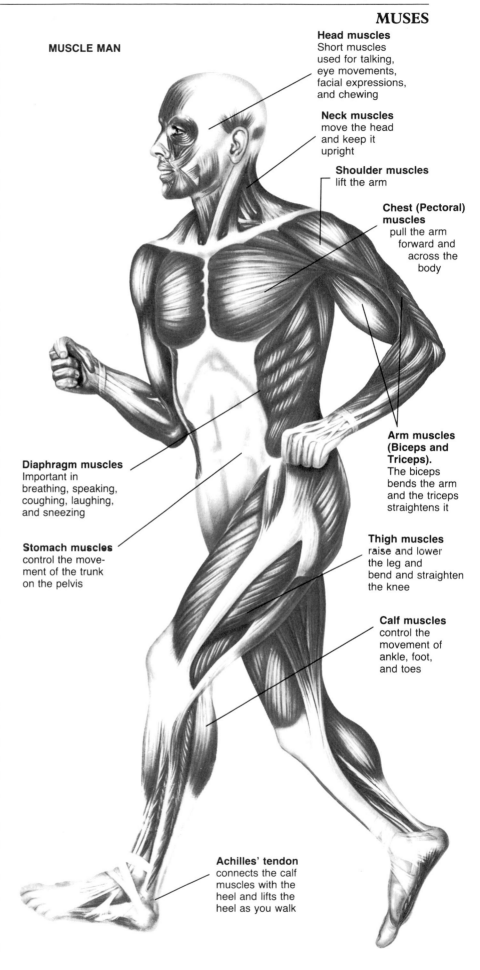

MUSCLE MAN

Head muscles
Short muscles used for talking, eye movements, facial expressions, and chewing

Neck muscles
move the head and keep it upright

Shoulder muscles
lift the arm

Chest (Pectoral) muscles
pull the arm forward and across the body

Arm muscles (Biceps and Triceps).
The biceps bends the arm and the triceps straightens it

Diaphragm muscles
Important in breathing, speaking, coughing, laughing, and sneezing

Stomach muscles
control the movement of the trunk on the pelvis

Thigh muscles
raise and lower the leg and bend and straighten the knee

Calf muscles
control the movement of ankle, foot, and toes

Achilles' tendon
connects the calf muscles with the heel and lifts the heel as you walk

▲ *Music, art, and poetry were held in high regard by the ancient Greeks. The goddesses of poetry and song were the Muses.*

a comic mask, was the Muse of comedy and pastoral poetry. Calliope, the most honored of all the Muses, carried a writing tablet and *stylus* (writing tool). She was the Muse of epic, or heroic, poetry. Euterpe, who played the flute, was the Muse of lyric poetry. Melpomene, who wore a tragic mask and carried a sword, was the Muse of tragedy. Erato, the Muse of love poetry, and Terpsichore, the Muse of dancing and singing, both carried stringed instruments called *lyres*. Polyhymnia, the Muse of sacred songs, or hymns, wore a veil over her face. Urania, the Muse of astronomy, was pictured with a globe. The ancient Greeks prayed to the Muses for inspiration before beginning any artistic, literary, or scientific project.

ALSO READ: GODS AND GODDESSES; GREECE, ANCIENT; MYTHOLOGY.

MUSEUM Have you ever wanted to see how prehistoric people or the colonial Americans lived? Did you ever wish you could go inside a submarine or see inside the tomb of an Egyptian pharaoh? You *can* see these things—at a museum.

Museums are places where great collections are kept. Perhaps you collect things, such as stamps, marbles, cards, coins, or model cars. Museums collect and take care of valuable art works, historical objects, and scientific objects. The director of a museum has several *curators* working under him or her. Each curator is in charge of a separate type of collection. The director and curators must get new items for the museum's collection. They do this by buying or trading with other museums or with people who have important objects to sell. Sometimes people who own valuable objects will give them to museums as a gift. Some museums that have a great deal of money send out scientific expeditions to find objects.

Museum workers keep records of every object in the collection. They number each object, write a detailed description of it, and photograph it. The description tells when, where, and how the object was found, the age and value of the object, and its importance.

Special museum workers called *conservators* clean each object and try to *restore* (repair) it by putting it back into good shape or working order. They also protect objects by treating and storing them safely.

Large museums do not show their whole collections at the same time. Only the most interesting or important objects are put on display. Most of the objects are stored away in *study collections* for scientists and historians to use. Study collections contain thousands of objects that are interesting only to experts in various subjects. The objects that are on display are grouped into *exhibits*. Dinosaur bones may be one kind of exhibit. American Indian life may be another. A *permanent exhibit* stays at one museum. A *temporary exhibit* is a special collection that is sent around to various museums. Each museum displays it for a short time and then sends it on to another museum. This gives peo-

▼ *A recent fossil find, a giant duck-billed dinosaur* Shantungosaurus, *is reconstructed and displayed in the Peking (Beijing) Natural History Museum.*

ple in many places a chance to see the exhibit. Some museums have small *traveling exhibits* that are sent to schools or communities of people who cannot come to the museum.

Museums have guides who take groups of visitors around. Guides explain the exhibits and tell the history and importance of the objects. Museum displays always have labels that tell something about the objects—their history, how they were used, who used them, and other interesting facts. Large museums give courses, in which you can learn about various historical or scientific subjects. Museums have speakers, usually experts in various fields, who give talks on interesting topics. Museums also show films and slides, and almost all museums have shops that sell photographs of some of the objects on display. Most of the large museums publish magazines to which you can subscribe.

Kinds of Museums HISTORY MUSEUMS. The museums collect objects that have important historical valuc. History muscums may be very large, dealing with the history of the entire world. Smaller museums have collections that show the history of a particular place, such as a nation, city, or state. Some history museums are based on the life of a particular person, event, or group of people. The Lenin Museum in Moscow has collected a great number of objects connected with the life of Nikolai Lenin. The Gettysburg Museum in Gettysburg, Pennsylvania, tells the history of a U. S. Civil War battle. The DuSable Museum in Chicago, Illinois, tells of the history of black people.

The Smithsonian Institution in Washington, D.C., consists of many museums. Among the exhibits in its National Museum of History and Technology are the gowns worn by the wives of U.S. Presidents, the original Star-Spangled Banner that flew

over Fort McHenry during the War of 1812, Morse's telegraph, automobiles, trains, stamps, and coins.

ART MUSEUMS. Art museums contain collections of paintings, sculpture, drawings, handicrafts, and photography. Smaller art museums often concentrate on one kind of art. They collect the artwork of a certain area, of a certain time in history, or of a certain group of people.

NATURAL HISTORY MUSEUMS. Some museums collect plants and animals of the past and the present. They also exhibit rocks and fossil animals that show the history of the Earth. The Field Museum of Natural History in Chicago, Illinois, is a very large museum divided into four sections—*anthropology* (the study of human beings), *botany* (the study of plants), *geology* (the study of the Earth), and *zoology* (the study of animals). The exhibits include lifesize figures of prehistoric people, the most complete collection of meteorites in the world, and animals of different countries shown in their environment. The National Museum of Anthropology in Mexico City has the largest collection based on people in the Mexican region.

SCIENCE MUSEUMS. These museums display industrial and scientific equipment and show how it is used.

▲ *The National Air and Space Museum in Washington D.C. houses some of the earliest airplanes, including* Wright-Flyer I *and the* Spirit of St. Louis *(right), as well as many of NASA's space rockets, capsules and satellites.*

▼ *A doll house in the National Museum of History and Technology, part of the Smithsonian Institution in Washington D.C.*

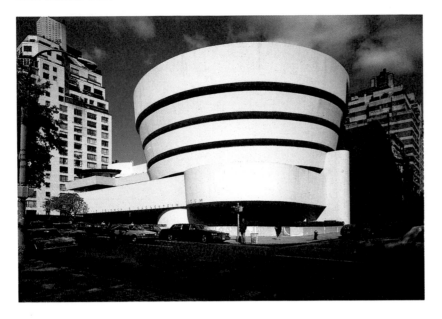

▲ *The Guggenheim Museum in New York City houses an art collection. The impressive circular building was designed by the architect Frank Lloyd Wright.*

At the Museum of Science and Industry in Chicago, Illinois, you can take a trip through a coal mine or see yourself on color television. You can climb aboard a full-sized submarine, stroll down a 1910 street, watch chickens hatch, or see how nuclear energy works.

OTHER MUSEUMS. *Children's museums* display children's collections, and the workers help children with hobbies. Children sometimes help take care of the museum. The museum director often takes groups of children on hikes or short "expeditions" to gather objects for a collection.

Folk museums are whole towns or groups of buildings that have been rebuilt or restored to their original condition. At a folk museum you can see how people of the past used to live. The town at Williamsburg, the colonial capital of Virginia, is a folk museum. You can walk through the old streets and into the buildings, houses, and shops. Guides dressed in colonial costume show you how Americans lived 250 years ago. Virginia City, Montana, is an old mining town of the middle 1800's that shows what life was like in the "Old West" during the gold rush.

Libraries can be museums, too. The big libraries in large cities have collections of ancient books and writings. The Library of Congress in Washington, D.C., has a copy of the Gutenberg Bible—the first book to be printed with movable type—and many other valuable writings.

If you travel to foreign countries, be sure to visit their museums. London has many museums of art and science. Paris has the Louvre, the world's greatest art museum. Leningrad has the Hermitage, and Madrid has the Padro.

ALSO READ: ART MUSEUMS AND GALLERIES, COLLECTING, ZOO.

MUSHROOM Mushrooms have been connected with magic for hundreds of years. This may be due to the way they grow. On a warm spring or summer morning, especially after a rain, people have found mushrooms growing where there were none the day before. They seem to appear as if by magic. Actually, there is nothing magical about mushrooms. They are members of a group of plants called *fungi*. They cannot make their own food because they do not contain the green chlorophyll that other types of plants have. Mushrooms get their food by causing vegetable matter to decay. For this reason, mushrooms, are often found growing on fallen logs as well as in the earth. Mushrooms are also called *toadstools*.

There are about 38,000 different kinds of mushrooms. They come in all colors except green, and they have a great number of shapes and sizes. The part of a mushroom that grows underground or in decaying wood is called the *mycelium*. It is much like a root because it holds the plant steady and takes in water and nourishment. Above ground is the mushroom stem, or *stipe*, topped by the cap. On the underside of the cap grow large numbers of *spores* on flat membranes called *gills*. Each spore acts like a seed. It drops to the ground and grows into a new mushroom plant

Mushrooms may range in height from about ¾ inch (1.9 cm) to about 15 inches (38 cm), with diameters of less than ¼ inch (0.6 cm) to about 18 inches (46 cm).

when the conditions are right.

Some mushrooms are good to eat, but other kinds are poisonous. The poisonous ones look very much like the nonpoisonous ones. The only way to tell them apart is to learn from an expert how to identify them.

Some types of mushrooms are grown for sale in stores. They are planted in caves, in dark, damp cellars, or in specially built mushroom houses where the temperature and moisture are kept just right. The mushrooms are grown in trays of decaying plant matter and manure, over which a layer of soil is spread. The mycelium is used for planting. In a few weeks, the spore-forming caps begin to appear. Several crops of mushrooms can be grown from one mycelium planting. As each crop is harvested, it is sent quickly to market. Mushrooms may also be dried and kept for a long time.

ALSO READ: FUNGUS, PLANT, POISON, POISONOUS PLANT.

MUSIC Music can be heard almost everywhere—on TV, radio, records, tapes, at church services, and in pa-

▼ *An Aymara Indian, from the region of Lake Titicaca in South America, plays his pipes, a musical instrument that dates back to Inca times.*

rades. Stores often have music playing to attract customers and make them feel comfortable. You can hear music at parties and dances, at football games, at concerts, at the ballet and even around a campfire.

Music has been a part of human life ever since the first civilizations began. Early people liked to hear the singing of birds, the sounds of flowing streams, the whispers and whistlings of the wind. They discovered that they could use their own voices to make musical sounds. No one knows when the first musical instruments were developed, but all ancient civilizations had various kinds of harps, horns, pipes, gongs, and drums. Music became a part of everyday life. People made up simple tunes as they worked and played. People made music for dancing and for religious ceremonies. None of this music was written down. It was passed along from generation to generation.

Music became so important in people's lives that formal music began to be written. Formal music is created by a composer for some special purpose or occasion. Composing and playing music became a special art. People listen to this type of music for its beauty and for what it communicates. Music developed differently in various parts of the world. Chinese, Indian, African, American Indian, or Middle Eastern music sounds very different from the music that developed in Western Europe.

Kinds of Music All music (classical, popular, folk, jazz, and the music of foreign lands) can be divided into two types—*vocal* and *instrumental*. Vocal music is sung either by one person or by a group. The most common type of vocal music is the song. *Operas* and *musical plays* are dramas in which many or all of the lines are sung instead of spoken. *Oratorios* and *cantatas* are stories told through music, but without stage acting.

Instrumental music is classified ac-

Crumble cap

Honey fungus

Death cap
DEADLY POISONOUS

Fly agaric
POISONOUS

▲ *Poisonous and nonpoisonous mushrooms can be hard to tell apart.*

▲ This ancient Egyptian wall painting shows a woman playing an early form of harp.

▼ A composer in the process of writing a piece of music. He picks out the notes on the piano as he puts the composition together.

cording to the number of musicians it takes to play it. *Solos* are played by one person. *Chamber music* is played by small groups of people. *Orchestral music* is played by a large number of people.

Sound in Music   Music is based on sound, but not just any sound. Music is sound put together and arranged to make listeners feel something. Music is a way of communicating through sounds, just as literature communicates through words, paintings communicate through lines and colors, and dances communicate through movements.

TONE.   Musical sounds are called *tones*. All tones are made by something vibrating. When you sing or hum, you create tones by forcing air between two vocal cords in your throat. Your vocal cords *vibrate* (move very rapidly back and forth) as your breath passes through. This vibration of your vocal cords makes your breath come out in sound waves that can be heard. In *stringed instruments* (such as guitars and violins), tones are made by plucking or drawing a bow over a tight string. This makes the string vibrate and causes the surrounding air to move in waves. In *percussion instruments* (such as drums, xylophones, cymbals, and pianos), tones are made by hitting a stretched skin, a piece of metal, or a tight string to make them vibrate. In *wind instruments* (such as trumpets, tubas, trombones, harmonicas, and flutes), tones are made by blowing air into the instruments in various ways.

■ **LEARN BY DOING**

PITCH.   Tones have certain *pitches* that are called "high" or "low." A high-pitched tone vibrates faster than a low-pitched tone. Hold a rubber band between your front teeth and pull it out in front of you with your left hand until it is tight. Pluck it several times and listen to the tone. Keep plucking and loosen the rubber band slowly by moving your left hand toward you. As the rubber band loosens, the pitch gets lower. When the rubber band is stretched tight, it vibrates faster and makes a higher-pitched tone. Next time you hear some music, listen carefully for the lower-pitched tones. They are sometimes harder to hear. ■

DURATION.   If you hum a tune, you will notice that some tones are held for a longer length of time than others. This is called *duration*. If all the tones were the same length, the music would not be very interesting. Hum several tunes (such as the "Star-Spangled Banner," "Jingle Bells," or "Row, Row, Row Your Boat") and tap your foot each time the tones change. Your tapping will not be even because not all the tones are the same length. You can also see that each tone has its own rhythm that comes from the arrangement of long and short tones.

INTENSITY.   Music is made not only by changing the pitch and duration of tones, but also by changing the *intensity*. Intensity is the loudness or softness of a tone. Listen carefully to any piece of music and try to hear the different intensities.

TONE QUALITY.   Tone quality is hard to explain in words, but it is easy to hear. The same tone sounds dif-

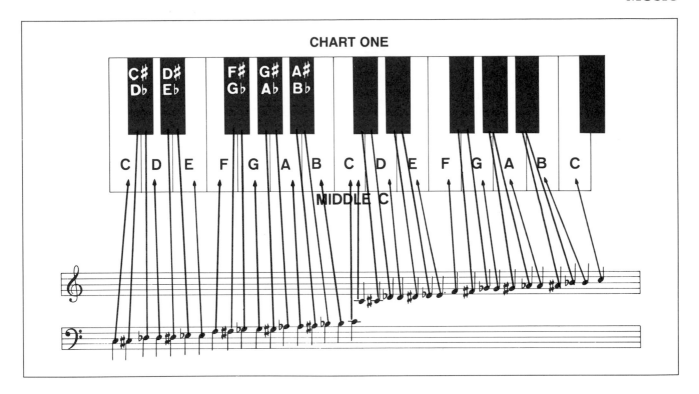

CHART ONE

ferent when played on a guitar and when played on a piano. The two instruments produce tones of different quality. The tone quality of a trumpet is different from the tone quality of a clarinet or a violin. When two people sing the same song, the tone quality of each voice is different. Listen to a recording of an orchestra or other music group and see how many different instruments you can recognize just by hearing the tone quality.

MELODY AND HARMONY. When composers write a tune, or *melody*, they select tones of different pitches and of various lengths and arrange them in a rhythm. They decide which parts of their melody will be louder and softer, and they choose the tone quality their melody will have by deciding the instruments to play it.

As composers create a melody, they also figure out the *harmony*. Harmony is made up of tones that fit with the melody. These tones support the melody and give the music a bigger, fuller, more interesting sound. Folk singers often sing a melody and play the harmony on a guitar, banjo, or other instrument. The harmony is

usually made up of *chords* (two or more notes that are played at the same time).

Musical Notation Many people have learned music "by ear"—listening to a tune and imitating it. Notation is a way of writing down music so it can be played or sung by anyone even if he or she has never heard the music before. There have been many ways of writing music down. The notation used in Asia is different from that used in the West. Medieval and Renaissance music was written in a notation different from that used today.

To read music, you must learn what the notes and other markings stand for. Musical notes are arranged from left to right on a *staff* that has five lines. The position of the round head of a note—on a line or on a space between lines—tells you the tone. (Chart One shows notes on a staff and the piano keys that the notes stand for.)

Tones are named by letters A through G of the alphabet. The tone called "middle C" is located at the center of the piano keyboard. Tones

Bones with holes in them have been found in the U.S.S.R. and Hungary. It is believed that they were used as primitive flutes. They have been dated at about 20,000 B.C.

CHART TWO

pitched higher than middle C are written on the top staff. On the left end of the top staff is a sign called *G-clef* (𝄞). This sign tells you that the tone G is written on the second line from the bottom. The *G-clef* spiral winds around that second line. Tones pitched lower than middle C are written on the bottom staff. The sign at the left end of the bottom staff is called the *F-clef* (𝄢). It tells you that the tone F is written on the fourth line from the bottom. The two dots of the F-clef sign are on both sides of that fourth line. Once you know where G is on the top staff and F is on the bottom staff, it's easy to figure out where the other notes should be placed.

Some notes have an extra sign in front of them. The ♯ sign means "sharp." The ♭ sign means "flat." A ♯ sign in front of a note means the tone is raised a half step. A ♭ sign means the tone is lowered a half step. On the piano, a half step is the next lower or higher key. Find the G note on the top staff, second line from the bottom. The notes just before and after G are on the same line, but one has a ♭ and the other has a ♯ sign. By following the arrows to the keyboard, you can see that G-sharp is played on the next higher key. G-flat is played on the next lower key.

■ LEARN BY DOING

Written music begins with a clef sign and the *key signature*, made up of sharp or flat signs that tell you in advance which notes will always be sharp or flat. The signs are placed on the lines or spaces of the notes that must be made sharp or flat. Can you figure out from the key signatures in Chart Two which notes will be sharp or flat? ■

The way each note is written tells you how long it is held. The top staff in Chart Three shows notes of different lengths. The *whole note* is held longest. The *half note* is held only half as long as the whole note. Two half notes equal a whole note. It takes four *quarter notes* to equal a whole note; eight *eighth notes* to equal a whole note; sixteen *sixteenth notes* to equal a whole note.

The second staff in Chart Three shows rests of different lengths. A *rest* means no sound—silence. The various rests tell you how long the silence is held.

The second and third staffs of Chart Three show two melodies. Lines crossing the staff from top to bottom divide the notes into groups, called *measures*. The first staff has four measures. How many does the second staff have? At the end of each staff is a

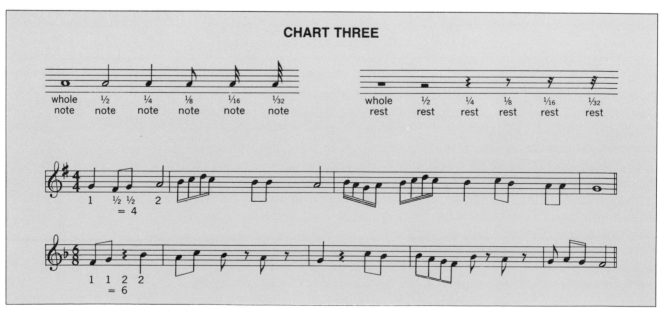

double line, called a *double bar*. The double bar shows the end of a piece of music. Both staffs have double bars—each staff is a separate piece of music.

The *time signature* is written after the key signature. The time signature has two numbers, one above the other. These numbers tell you what the rhythm, or beat, will be. The top number tells you how many beats are in each measure. The bottom number tells you which kind of note receives one beat. The time signature on the first melody has a 4 on the bottom. This means that a quarter (¼) note receives one beat. (Notice that only the bottom number of the fraction ¼ is used in the time signature.) The time signature of the second melody has an 8 on the bottom. This means that an eighth (⅛) note (♪) receives one beat. With a time signature of 4/4, the notes and rests in each measure must add up to four beats. With a time signature of 6/8, the notes and rests in each measure must add up to six beats. You can test this yourself by adding up the beats in each measure.

Musicians A person who plays music just for enjoyment is called an *amateur* musician. If a person earns a living in the field of music, he or she is a *professional* musician. Amateurs sing in choirs; play in bands, orchestras, and small groups; or they play music for their own pleasure at home.

Professional musicians are members of symphony orchestras, military bands, dance bands, and jazz or rock groups. They are concert singers and instrumentalists and teachers of music. They are composers who create music for performance. *Musicologists* study the history and scientific aspects of music.

■ **LEARN BY DOING**

To enjoy music, all you have to do is listen to it. Try to hear all the sounds and rhythms. Pay attention to how the sounds fit together and move. Is the music fast and tricky or

GLOSSARY OF MUSICAL TERMS
KINDS OF CLASSICAL MUSIC

Aria A melody or song sung by only one person. An aria is usually part of an opera or choral work.
Ballade A short piece of music, usually for the piano, based on the ideas and feelings of a poem.
Chorale A musical piece for choir or organ based on a hymn tune.
Concerto A large musical work for one instrument or a small group of instruments with orchestra accompaniment. Most concertos have three movements with a cadenza in each.
Dance forms Pieces for one or more instruments based on dance rhythms. The *waltz, minuet, polka, gigue* (or *jig*), *polonaise, mazurka, pavan,* and *sarabande* are examples of dance forms.
Etude A short musical piece written to help a player practice his or her instrument.
Finale The concluding movement of a long musical work.
Fugue A musical piece in which one or more melodies are played in a certain order and then repeated in different pitches or varied in other ways.
Madrigal A song for two to six voices, based on romantic or love poetry and sung in parts without accompaniment.
March A musical piece for marching, usually played by a band.
Motet A musical piece for voices, usually sung in parts without accompaniment and based on religious or sacred texts.
Nocturne A dreamy, romantic musical piece connected with a mood or idea about night.
Overture A musical piece written as an introduction to a longer work, such as an opera.
Prelude A name given to any short instrumental piece. A prelude is usually written as an introduction to an instrumental piece of a different type.
Rondo A musical composition having a theme that is repeated at least three times between other sections.
Sonata A musical piece in three or four movements, usually played by one or two instruments.
Suite An instrumental composition that contains a series of dances.
Symphony A large musical composition of three or four movements played by an orchestra. A symphony is a sonata for orchestra. *Symphony* is also another name for an orchestra.
Theme and variations An instrumental composition in which one theme, or melody, is played in many different ways.
Tone poem An orchestral work written to express a mood or tell a romantic story.

CLASSICAL MUSICAL COMPOSITION

A cappella Without instrumental accompaniment.
Accompaniment A musical part that is played along with a solo part and that supports it.
Cadenza A section of music in a concerto played by the soloist alone. A cadenza is always very difficult to play and gives the soloist a chance to show off his or her skill.
Chorus or refrain A phrase or theme that is repeated after each verse of a song.
Composition Any musical piece or work.
Counterpoint Two or more melodies that are written to be played at the same time.
Key The name of the scale on which a musical composition is based.
Motif A very short theme, melody, or phrase around which a musical composition is developed.
Movement A section of a longer instrumental work, such as a concerto, sonata, or symphony.
Octave Two tones, one having twice as many vibrations a second as the other. The tones of a scale fit within an octave.

GLOSSARY CONTINUES OVERLEAF

GLOSSARY OF MUSICAL TERMS CONTINUED

Scale A series of tones each of which is higher or lower in pitch than the one before. The tones of the 7-tone scale progress in a definite pattern of half steps and whole steps that establishes the key. In the 12-tone scale, also called the *chromatic scale*, all tones are a half step apart.

Solo A musical composition for one voice or instrument, with or without accompaniment.

Tempo The speed at which a musical composition is played or sung.

Theme A melody used as the basis for a musical composition.

PLAYING CLASSICAL MUSIC

Tempo markings Words that tell a musician how fast or slow a piece should be played.

Adagio Slow tempo.
Allegretto Medium-quick tempo.
Allegro Fast tempo.
Andante Medium-slow tempo.
Largo Very slow, solemn tempo.
Presto Very fast tempo.

Dynamic markings Words and signs that tell a musician how loud or soft the music should be played.

Crescendo (⊂) Gradually louder.
Decrescendo or **Diminuendo (⊃)** Gradually softer.
Forte (f) Loudly.
Fortissimo (ff) Very loud and forceful.
Mezzoforte (mf) Medium-loud.
Pianissimo (pp) Very soft and quiet.
Piano (p) Softly.
Sforzando (sf or sfz) Suddenly loud.

Style markings Words or signs that tell a musician how notes should be played.

Legato Smoothly, flowing together.
Marcato (╷ ╷) Each note separate.
Staccato (╵ ╵) Detached. Played short and sharp.

TYPES OF CLASSICAL MUSICIANS

Composer A person who creates musical works.
Concertmaster The first violinist and assistant conductor in a symphony orchestra.
Conductor A person who directs a musical group.
Prima donna The leading female soloist in an opera.
Virtuoso A musician who has very great skill and can perform very difficult music brilliantly.

MISCELLANEOUS

Baton A stick used by a conductor when directing.
Concert A musical performance.
Manuscript A piece of unprinted music, usually written in the composer's own handwriting.
Metronome A small machine that can be made to tick at various rates of speed. By practicing with a metronome, a musician can keep a steady beat in his or her music.
Musicology The historical and scientific study of music.
Mute A device for softening the tone of an instrument.
Opus A musical composition. The Latin word *opus* is used with a number (Opus 15, Opus 110, etc.) to show the order in which a composer's works were written or published.
Score A printed musical composition containing all the parts or containing only the part for a particular instrument or voice.
Sight reading Reading and performing music without studying it beforehand.
Tuning Adjusting a musical instrument so that it produces the correct pitch.
Tuning fork A small, metal instrument with two prongs. When it is struck, the fork vibrates to produce a particular pitch by which instruments can be tuned.

slow and quiet? Is it loud like a scream or whispery like a breeze? Is it deep like a roll of thunder or ringing like a bell? How does the music make you feel—proud, sad, spooky, peaceful, nervous, funny, excited?

People like music because it communicates something to them. If a piece of music communicates well and remains interesting, it is considered "good music." A piece of music that is well written can be heard over and over again. It doesn't "wear out" or get boring. *Classical music* is a name given to musical works that have remained interesting to people for a long time. Most *popular music* is music that people like for a while, but after a time most of it "wears out."

As you listen to more and more music, you get to know how music communicates. If a piece of music seems boring at first, put it aside and listen to it later. Try exploring different kinds of music, instead of just listening to the things you like. It takes time to listen to new music. You may not like it at first, but give the music a chance.

After listening to music, try singing or playing music yourself. Many schools have free music programs where you can learn to play an instrument or sing well. Visit a music store and examine the instruments and the printed music. Many music stores have teachers who give music lessons. Libraries have books on music and records and tapes. ■

For further information on:
Composers, *see Index at name.*
Elements of Music, *see* HEARING, SOUND, TIME.
Kinds of Music, *see* BALLET, CAROL, CHORAL MUSIC, DANCE, ELECTRONIC MUSIC, FOLK SONG, JAZZ, MUSICAL COMEDY, OPERA, POPULAR MUSIC.
Musical Instruments, *see* ACCORDION, BAGPIPE, BELL, BRASS INSTRUMENTS, CALLIOPE, HARMONICA, HARP, MUSICAL INSTRUMENTS, MUSIC BOX, ORGAN, PERCUSSION INSTRUMENTS,

PIANO, STRINGED INSTRUMENTS, WOODWIND INSTRUMENTS, XYLOPHONE.

Music Groups, *see* CHORUSES AND CHOIRS, ORCHESTRAS AND BANDS, SINGING.

Musicians, *see* ANDERSON, MARIAN; ARMSTRONG, LOUIS; CAREERS; CARUSO, ENRICO; HANDY, WILLIAM C.; JACKSON, MAHALIA; SCHWEITZER, ALBERT.

Recording Music, *see* COMPACT DISC, RECORDING, TAPE RECORDER.

MUSICAL COMEDY Early in the 20th century a new kind of musical stage show, called musical comedy, developed in the United States. George M. Cohan's *Little Johnny Jones* is an early example. *Hello, Dolly!* by Jerry Herman and Michael Stewart is a very popular one.

Musical comedy puts together song, dance, and spoken dialogue to create a musical play. Musical comedy shows the influence of European operettas, or light operas, especially those by Gilbert and Sullivan. American operettas, such as those by Victor Herbert, Sigmund Romberg, and Rudolf Friml, also led to the development of musical comedy. It was also influenced by vaudeville and revues, in which many unconnected songs, dance numbers, and bits of comedy were strung into an evening's entertainment. A musical comedy has a plot, and the songs and dances are all connected to it. In the 1940's a new style for musical comedy was set with the production of *Oklahoma!* by Richard Rodgers and Oscar Hammerstein II. It presented a unique combination of songs and *choreography* (specially created dances) suitable for its setting—the early days of Oklahoma.

Musical comedies were only stage shows at first. Since the 1930's, a great many successful musicals have been made into movies. Since movies get larger audiences, they have made musical comedies even more popular than they were before.

Musical comedies, as an American form of entertainment, often take their subjects from America's present or past. The earliest musical comedies by George M. Cohan are noted for their extremely patriotic, American subjects. *Annie, Get Your Gun* by Irving Berlin and Herbert and Dorothy Fields and *Oklahoma!* are based on the Old West. *Funny Girl* by Jule Styne, Isobel Lennart, and Bob Merrill is based on the life of Fannie Brice, an American comedienne in the early part of this century. *The Music Man* by Meredith Willson is an affectionate look at life in the American Midwest in the early 1900's. *Guys and Dolls* by Abe Burrows and Frank Loesser is based on stories about small-time American gamblers in the 1920's.

Many musical comedies were adapted from works of literature—novels, stories, or nonmusical plays. *South Pacific* by Rodgers and Hammerstein is based on stories about World War II by James Michener. *My Fair Lady* is a musical version of the play *Pygmalion* by George Bernard Shaw. Shakespeare's play *The Taming of the Shrew* inspired the musical *Kiss Me, Kate* by Cole Porter and Sam and Bella Spewack. *Mame* is based on a popular novel, written by

▲ *Richard Rodgers, an accomplished American composer, wrote the music for such popular musicals as Oklahoma!, South Pacific, and The Sound of Music.*

▼ *A scene from* My Fair Lady, *a musical comedy composed by Frederick Loewe, and adapted from George Bernard Shaw's play* Pygmalion.

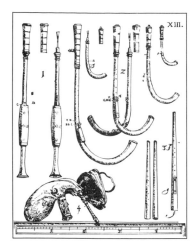

▲ *Illustrations published in 1618, showing three "families" of musical instruments. Top: Shawms, crumhorns, cornetts, and bagpipes; Center: Members of the string family; Bottom: Drums.*

Patrick Dennis, about a boy's very unusual and lovable aunt. *The Matchmaker*, a successful play by Thornton Wilder, provided the basis for *Hello, Dolly!* Shakespeare's tragedy *Romeo and Juliet* inspired a musical about two young lovers in New York's slums, *West Side Story* by Leonard Bernstein. *Man of La Mancha* by Dale Wasserman, Joe Darion, and Mitch Leigh is taken from Miguel de Cervantes's story of Don Quixote, an impractical old man who was convinced that he was a knight. He clung to his belief that people were noble and good, even though everyone made fun of him.

This musical, like many others, is not really a comedy. In the 1930's *Of Thee I Sing* by George and Ira Gershwin, George S. Kaufman, and Morris Ryskind offered the public a serious satire of American politics in a musical comedy. It was the first musical comedy to win a Pulitzer Prize. In the 1940's *Pal Joey* by Richard Rodgers, Lorenz Hart, and John O'Hara presented realistic characters in the lighthearted, musical-comedy manner. In the 1960's several popular musicals presented serious ideas as well as good entertainment. *Fiddler on the Roof* by Jerry Bock, Sheldon Harnick, and Joseph Stein tells a story of the courage of a group of Russian Jewish peasants. *Cabaret* by John Kander, Fred Ebb, and Joe Masteroff describes conditions in Berlin just before Hitler's dictatorship began.

Other musicals are based on sheer fantasy, or imagination. *Brigadoon* by Alan Jay Lerner and Frederick Loewe is a love story set in a little Scottish town that appears once every hundred years, only to disappear after one day! *Finian's Rainbow* by Burton Lane, E. Y. Harburg, and Fred Saidy is the story of a search for leprechaun gold.

Songs from musicals are often so popular that they become familiar to people all over the country, even

those who never saw the show. "I'm a Yankee Doodle Dandy," written by George M. Cohan when your grandparents were children, is still occasionally sung today. "Some Enchanted Evening" from *South Pacific* and "I Could Have Danced All Night" from *My Fair Lady* are familiar to many people. And you may still hear "My Funny Valentine" from *Pal Joey* on the radio on February 14.

From the mid-1970's to the mid-1980's, several new musicals have been very successful. *A Chorus Line* by James Kirkwood and Nicholas Dante shows the continual struggles of young dancers who wish to make a career in the theater. *Evita* by Timothy Rice and Andrew Lloyd Webber presents the rise and fall of the former Argentine political leader, Eva Perón. *Annie* by Martin Charnin is a happy musical comedy, despite its setting during the hard times of the Depression. Later came *Les Misérables*, adapted from the novel by Victor Hugo, and *The Phantom of the Opera*.

ALSO READ: COHAN, GEORGE M.; GERSHWIN, GEORGE AND IRA; POPULAR MUSIC.

MUSICAL INSTRUMENTS
Musical instruments are devices for making musical sounds, or tones. Instruments may be very simple, such as animal skin stretched over a frame to make a drum. Huge church organs are very complicated, with many keyboards and hundreds of pipes. The guitar, piano, and harmonica are familiar instruments, but others, such as the Japanese *koto*, the East Indian *sitar*, and the Russian *balalaika*, are not as well known to us.

All musical instruments are divided into three groups according to how the tone is produced. In *stringed instruments*, such as guitars and violins, tones are made by plucking or drawing a bow over a tight string. In *percussion instruments*, such as drums, xylophones, and pianos, tones are made by hitting a stretched skin, a piece of metal or wood, or a tight string. In *wind instruments*, such as trumpets or clarinets, tones are made by blowing air into the instruments in various ways.

There are two kinds of wind instruments—*woodwinds* and *brass*. The woodwinds (clarinets, flutes, piccolos, oboes, bassoons, and English horns) were once all made from wood. The brass instruments (trumpets, trombones, tubas, French horns, cornets, saxophones, bugles) are all made of metal.

When a musical instrument is plucked, bowed, hit, or blown into, vibrations are set up. The vibrations cause the surrounding air to move in sound waves that can be heard.

Each musical instrument has its own special kind of sound, called *tone quality* or *timbre*. The same tune sounds different when played on a trumpet, violin, flute, or guitar. A melody played on a bassoon will sound very deep and resonant. The same melody played on a piccolo will sound very high in pitch and perhaps even shrill. You can test the timbre of a grand piano by placing a cloth at different points over the strings and then striking the keys. The sound will be full and rich without the cloth. The tone quality is determined partly by an instrument's *resonance*. As an instrument is played, the vibrations are picked up by the whole body of the instrument. When you pluck a guitar, for example, the vibrations of the strings cause the wooden body of the instrument to vibrate, too. This kind of vibration is called *resonance*.

■ LEARN BY DOING

Materials have various kinds of resonance. You can test this yourself. Use a spoon to tap objects such as a glass, a plate, a metal pan, a wooden bowl, a hard plastic dish, and a piece of cloth. Hold each object lightly at one edge. As you tap, listen to the quality of the sounds. The cloth has the least resonance. It does not pick up vibrations well and tapping it only makes a dull thud. Wood, metal, and glass are good resonators. They pick up vibrations easily and continue to vibrate for quite a long time. Glass is too breakable and is not generally used in making instruments. All the stringed instruments and many percussion and woodwind instruments are made of wood. Metals are used in most others. Various metals and woods resonate differently, which is one reason why instruments have different tone qualities. ■

Musical instruments differ in pitch. Some can produce very high tones.

▲ *A Baroque instrument maker and his wares.*

The musical note most commonly used to check the tuning of musical instruments is *A*. It is usually played by the oboe before a performance. The oboe is chosen because it has a very steady pitch.

◀ *In a modern symphony orchestra, the instruments are arranged in groups, with the strings at the front and brass and percussion (drums and cymbals) at the back.*

Fidla (board zither), Iceland

Hardanger fiddle, Nor

Pianoforte
Western
Europe

Terracotta fipple flute,
Portugal

Rebab (fi
North Afr

Double horn
Morocco

Bow harp, Senegal

Alghaita (shaw
Nigeria

Barrel dru
Ghana

Four-toned whistle, British
Columbia

Gourd rattle, North America

Frame drum, North America

Leather rattle,
North America

Spur jingle, North America

Appalachian dulcimer, North
America

Papago (wood scraper),
North America

Slit drum, Mexico

Long drum, Haiti

Marimba, Guatemala

Bird-bone flutes,
Panama

Steel drum, Trinidad

Multiple flute,
Ecuador

End-blown flute, British
Guiana

Pan pipes, Peru

Wooden bull-roarer, Brazil

Clay trumpet,
Peru

Jingle, South America

Animal horn, Bolivia

Tortoise shell friction drum

Shawm, Middle East

Multiple pipe, South America

Portative organ,
Medieval Europe

Trumpet, Ancient Egypt

Tromba marine,
Medieval Europe

Angle harp, U.S.S.R.

Nyckelharpa, Sweden

owed zither, Germany

Bird-scare clapper,
U.S.S.R.

Fandur
(olk fiddle),
U.S.S.R.

Saddle chime bells, U.S.S.R.

Animal horn, U.S.S.R.

Violin, Italy

Crescent jingle, Turkey

Kemange (spike fiddle), Iran

Folk shawm, Tibet

Wind bell, Korea

Wooden *tsuri daiko* (drum),
Japan

Bamboo and wood *shô*
(mouth organ), Japan

Okedo (drum), Japan

Ko-kiu (fiddle), Japan

'Ud (lute), Syria

ane double
rinet, Egypt

Bagpipe, Arabia

Sitar (lute), India

Large trumpet, Burma

Bamboo *ti-tzu* (flute),
China

Cymbals, China

Saw-thai (spike fiddle),
Thailand

Tam âm la (chime) Vietnam

Sistrum (rattle), Ethiopia

Jew's
harp, India

Ranasringa
(horn), India

Chakay (zither), Thailand

Angle harp,
Congo

Kerar
(lyre),
Ethiopia

Bagana (lyre), Ethiopia

Veena (lute), India

Bamboo and gourd mouth
organ, Borneo

Gong chime, Borneo

Scraper, East Africa

Basketwork clapper, Congo

Shawm, Java

Gansa (metallophone), Bali

Horn, South Africa

ussion
d,
a

Zither, Madagascar

Hurdy-gurdy,
Medieval Europe

Wooden bull-roarer,
Australia

Ombgwe (vessel flute),
South Africa

Maori *putorino* (trumpet),
New Zealand

Psaltery, Near East

▲ *Classical violinist Yehudi Menuhin promoted works of contemporary composers and revived valuable music of the past.*

▼ *Pop music has adapted traditional instruments such as the piano and guitar and amplified their sounds electronically. Electronic synthesizers have added a range of new sounds to pop music.*

Others make very low tones. The size of an instrument is a good way to tell its pitch. Smaller instruments produce higher pitches, and larger instruments produce lower pitches. The big tubas, bass viols, and double bassoons can reach way down to tones much lower than anyone can sing. The trumpet, violin, and tiny piccolo can make tones that are higher than any voice can sing. Some instruments, such as the piano, harp, and organ, can play a wide range of pitches.

A symphony orchestra has instruments that can play the highest and lowest of musical tones. It contains instruments of various tone qualities, and it has instruments that can play very loudly or very softly. Instruments that are not usually found in an orchestra are used in other types of performances. Guitars, banjos, accordians, and harmonicas are used to accompany singing. More ancient instruments, such as recorders, are played in small groups.

No one knows exactly when the first musical instruments were developed. One of the earliest was the musical bow, much like a hunter's bow. Its one string was plucked as it

▲ *Trumpets (top) are brass wind instruments. The flute (bottom) is a woodwind, though most modern flutes are metal. Early flutes were made of wood.*

was made tighter or looser to change the pitch. Early people made rattles from dried reeds, drums from hollow logs, and simple pipes from bamboo stalks. All early civilizations had developed various kinds of harps, horns, pipes, gongs, and drums. The ancient Greeks even invented a complicated organ, called a *hydraulus*, that was run by water.

Over the years, instruments have changed in shape, size, and tone quality, but the ways they are played—hitting, blowing, plucking, and drawing a bow—have stayed the same. In the 1940's and 1950's, musicians began to experiment with new kinds of instruments that produce sounds electronically. These instruments include the electric guitar, electric bass, and electric piano. There is also the synthesizer which uses solid-state cir-

cuitry and keyboards to produce the sounds of other musical instruments and even whole orchestras. Making the sound of instruments larger and louder by hooking them to amplifiers and loudspeakers is another recent change. Mini-computers are also used to enhance the range of tones and aid tuning.

ALSO READ: ACCORDION, BAGPIPE, BELL, BRASS INSTRUMENTS, CALLIOPE, ELECTRONIC MUSIC, HARMONICA, HARP, HEARING, MUSIC, ORCHESTRAS AND BANDS, ORGAN, PERCUSSION INSTRUMENTS, PIANO, SOUND, STRINGED INSTRUMENTS, WOODWIND INSTRUMENTS, XYLOPHONE.

MUSICAL NOTE see MUSIC.

MUSIC BOX People for many years enjoyed the delicate music produced by music boxes. A music box contains a mechanism that plays a tune. The mechanism is usually contained in a small box, but music boxes have also been built into large objects, such as desks and ornate, moving clocks. Some music boxes can play very complicated and delicate music.

A music box consists of a brass cylinder or barrel, with metal pins sticking out of the sides. The cylinder is turned by clockwork. As it turns, the pins pluck the teeth of a metal comb. The teeth of the comb produce the tinkling tones. The *barrel organ*, played by wandering musicians in the Middle Ages and still played in the streets of some cities today, has this kind of mechanism. The cylinder of a barrel organ is turned by a hand crank.

A music box was sent by Queen Elizabeth I of England as a gift to the Sultan of Turkey in 1593. Music boxes were not widely known until the 1700's and 1800's. Switzerland became famous for making music boxes. Some of the most popular music boxes today still come from Swit-

zerland. In France, music boxes with elaborate moving figures, or *automatons*, were made. The figures danced in time with the music. A funny music box in the form of a *bustle* (a pad worn at the back of a dress) was presented to Queen Victoria of Great Britain. If she sat down while wearing this bustle, the music box inside played "God Save the Queen." The Austrian composer, Franz Joseph Haydn, wrote several tunes for music boxes.

MUSLIM see ISLAM.

MUSSEL see CLAMS AND OYSTERS.

MUSSOLINI, BENITO (1883–1945) Benito Mussolini was the founder of the Fascist Party in Italy. He was the dictator of Italy for over 20 years.

The Italian people had suffered very much during World War I, even though Italy was on the winning side. Born in Romagna province, Benito Mussolini had been a revolutionary Socialist and a newspaper editor before the war. He fought in the war and was wounded and decorated. In

▲ *Antique, decorative music boxes such as this are treasured by collectors. The cylinder is turned by a special clock which is wound by the handle (left). As it turns, the tiny pins on the cylinder pluck teeth on a metal comb at the front.*

When the German resistance in Italy collapsed in April 1945, Mussolini and a few followers tried to escape from the Allied advance. They were seized near Como by Italian resistance fighters and shot. Mussolini's body was taken to Milan and hung head downward from a lamp post in the Piazza Loreto.

▲ *A rare color picture showing the Italian dictator Mussolini reviewing his troops.*

▼ *William Bligh, a British naval officer, who achieved notoriety as the commander of the* Bounty. *The book,* Mutiny on the Bounty, *written in 1932, tells of the adventures of the* Bounty *crew. Marlon Brando starred in the 1962 movie version of the book.*

1919, Mussolini founded a political organization called the Fascist Party, which violently opposed the Communists. Mussolini's followers called him *Il Duce* ("the leader"). Mussolini promised the Italian people that he would make Italy strong and prosperous if his Fascist Party were elected to office.

Many Italian people believed Mussolini and supported him. On October 28, 1922, Mussolini's followers, called the Black Shirts, marched on the city of Rome. They demanded that the king of Italy, Victor Emmanuel III, put Mussolini in charge of the government. The king made Mussolini prime minister.

Mussolini soon seized all power for himself and turned the Italian government into a dictatorship. He destroyed the Communist, Socialist, and other political organizations, and imprisoned and tortured people who disagreed with him. But he also began a program to improve Italy's economy. He built new roads and encouraged the growth of industry, which gave the people more jobs. Mussolini wanted to make Italy a powerful country. He sent Italian armies to conquer Ethiopia (1935) and to help General Francisco Franco fight

against the republican government in Spain (1936).

World War II broke out in 1939. Mussolini finally allied Italy formally with the German side when France was near collapse (1940). When Italy was conquered by American and British troops, Mussolini tried to escape to Germany. He was captured and killed by Italian resistance fighters on April 28, 1945.

ALSO READ: DICTATOR, FASCISM, ITALIAN HISTORY, WORLD WAR II.

MUTATION see EVOLUTION, GENETICS.

MUTINY A mutiny is a rebellion against military authority by military personnel, such as soldiers or sailors. A mutiny may simply be a refusal of the men and women to follow the orders given by their commanders, or it may be actual armed combat of people against their commanders. During a war, mutiny could result in loss of lives or capture by the enemy. For this reason, military law usually provides strict punishment for convicted mutineers.

U.S. military law defines mutiny not only as an open rebellion. Mutiny can be hidden acts of rebellion (such as illegally storing up ammunition for use against officers and commanders). Persons who know about these hidden acts and do not try to stop them are also guilty of mutiny. Mutineers who are found guilty may be punished by fine and imprisonment. In cases of serious mutiny where there has been loss of life, they may be sentenced to death.

Perhaps the best-known mutiny was that which occurred on the British naval ship, the *Bounty*. In 1789, the ship was on an exploratory voyage in the South Pacific. The captain, William Bligh, was an experienced seaman and knew a great deal about navigation. But he was fierce, brutal, and unjust in his treatment of the crew. The first mate, Fletcher Christian, led a revolt against the ruthless captain and took command of the *Bounty*. He set Captain Bligh and some of Bligh's officers adrift in a small boat with a few days' food supply. The little boat sailed nearly 4,000 miles (6,500 km) before the captain and his officers were rescued. Meanwhile, Fletcher Christian and some of the mutineers set up a colony on Pitcairn Island in the South Pacific. Others of the mutineers were caught and later executed in England.

ALSO READ: COURT SYSTEM, LAW.

MYCENAE   see GREECE, ANCIENT.

MYTHOLOGY   In ancient times, most people believed that the world and the universe were inhabited by many different gods and spirits. The sun was often thought to be a god, and the moon a goddess. The winds and the rain were gods, and people worshiped gods and goddesses, or *deities*, of the sea, wine, and hunting. There were gods of thunder and war, and gentler gods of love, marriage, and the countryside. The stories that tell of the gods and their deeds are called *myths*. The study of myths is known as mythology.

To those ancient peoples, myths were not just entertaining stories, but part of their religion. People prayed to their gods and tried to behave in ways that they thought would please the gods. In those early times, people did not have all the scientific knowledge we have today. If a river flooded its banks, they thought it was caused by an evil or angry god. People did not understand nature's ways. So they made up the gods and the marvelous stories called myths to explain the natural happenings. Some myths are also about extraordinary human beings, who perform great deeds. These human beings are called *heroes*. Some mythical beings are *demigods* (half gods), with one parent a god or goddess and the other a mortal (human being). Myths tell of horrible, fire-breathing monsters, magic weapons, and fantastic animals that fly. They tell of the powers of the gods and the tricks they play on ordinary mortals.

The Myths of Many Peoples   Students of mythology have discovered myths all over the world. Ancient Babylonia, Persia, Egypt, and India had myths. American Indians told myths around their campfires. The peoples of the British Isles had their own mythology. In northern Europe, the Norse people created a lively collection of myths. But of all the recorded myths, those of Greece and Rome have become the most familiar. Many of these myths are about the most important gods and goddesses who lived on Mount Olympus. Greek myths tell of fabulous adventures and incredible feats. They contain love stories, both happy and sad, and sav-

▲ *Theseus, a heroic king in Greek mythology, killed the Minotaur, an ugly monster which had the body of a man and the head of a bull.*

NORSE GODS AND GODDESSES

The many gods and goddesses who lived in the icy land of Asgard were:

Odin   leader of the gods; also god of war, wind, and magic.
Frigg   goddess of marriage and the home, wife of Odin.
Thor   Odin's son, god of thunder and fire.
Balder   Odin's son, god of the sun and light.
Nanna   goddess of the moon, Balder's wife.
Frey   god of sunshine, rain, and fruit.
Freya   goddess of love, music, flowers, healing, and spring.
Njordhr   god of fertility and the sea.
Hel   goddess of the dead and the underworld.
Bragi   Odin's son, god of poetry and wisdom.
Idun   goddess of eternal youth and spring, Bragi's wife.
Tyr   Odin's son, god of athletics and battles.
Jord   goddess of earth.
Vithar   Odin's son, god of silence.
Ulle   god of hunting.
Hoder   Odin's son, blind god of winter months.
Bali   Odin's son.
Loki   god of evil, fraud, and mischief.
Thiassi   god of winter.
Ran   goddess of the deepest oceans.
Heimdall   watchman of the rainbow bridge.

▲ *A Greek coin of the 300's* B.C. *with an imaginary portrait of the poet Homer. Homer's long epic poems, the* Iliad *and the* Odyssey, *have added much to the rich mythology that has come down to us from ancient Greece.*

age battles involving heroic mortals or angry gods.

For many centuries, myths were handed down by word of mouth. One of the first persons to record the Greek myths in writing was a Greek poet named Hesiod. He lived around 800 years before the time of Jesus Christ. The mythology he recorded centers around the gods that lived on Mount Olympus. They were ruled by Zeus, who was chosen by the gods and goddesses after their final defeat of the Titans, an earlier group of divinities.

Greek heroes were nearly as important as gods. They were mortal, though some had gods as ancestors. Homer, another Greek poet, included deeds of both gods and heroes in the *Iliad* and the *Odyssey*, his long epic poems about the Trojan War. The heroes involved included Agamemnon, Odysseus, Achilles, Hector, and Paris.

Myths are much alike throughout the world. One reason for this may be that people in different parts of the world were puzzled by the same acts of nature, such as floods, storms, or the actions of the sun and moon. In this way, the myths invented in one land were very much like those of other lands. People adopted, or took over, other people's myths. Many of the Greek myths, for example, were adopted by the Romans. The Romans were a strong, warlike people who built mighty walls, roads, buildings, and cities. But they greatly admired the learning of the Greeks. So they began to tell stories about their own gods similar to those they had heard in the Greek myths. They even adopted some Greek gods into their own group of deities. One of these was Apollo, god of the sun.

Norse Myths Many centuries ago, the Norse peoples of Scandinavia told fantastic tales of gods, monsters, and heroes. Many of the Norse people were fierce pirates called Vikings, whose raiding ships sailed as far as Iceland and North America. Norse gods lived in a marvelous land called Asgard. One-eyed Odin, the leader of the Norse gods, lived in a palace named Valhalla. Odin was often accompanied by the Valkyries, 13 fiery maidens who decided which heroes should die on the battlefield. Frigg, goddess of marriage, was Odin's wife. Norse myths tell of battles between the gods, who were brave and just, and the giants, who were evil. The Icelandic people were the first to write down the Norse myths in two collections of stories called *Eddas*. The *Elder*, or *Poetic*, *Edda* contains over 30 poem-tales. No one knows who wrote them or exactly when. The *Younger*, or *Prose*, *Edda* was written by a famed Icelandic poet, called Snorri Sturluson, in the 1200's.

Other Norse myths were contained in colorful stories, called *sagas*. Many of these were written by Icelandic poets called *skalds*, also around A.D. 1200. Sagas were written for special

▼ *A bronze head of Apollo, best known as the sun god. He was also god of the arts that made men civilized and of the plagues that destroyed them.*

festive occasions. They told about real happenings, and of heroes who really lived, such as the great Norwegian king, Saint Olaf.

The greatest of all is the *Volsunga Saga*, the story of a heroic race of people called the Volsungs. A German myth called *Nibelungenlied* ("Song of the Nibelungs") is almost the same as the Volsunga Saga. The German composer Richard Wagner wrote four great operas based on this story. They include *Die Walküre* ("The Valkyrie") and *Götterdämerung* ("The Twilight of the Gods").

Mythology in Our World Today
People today still enjoy reading ancient myths even if they no longer believe them to be true. And mythology is still very much part of our everyday lives. The names of the months and the days of the week came from the Romans and the Norse people. March derives from Mars, the Roman god of war, and Thursday is from Thor, the Norse god of thunder. Many of the names used in the United States space program have been taken from mythology. For example, the Apollo program was named for the Greek sun god, and the mighty Saturn rocket bore the name of the Roman harvest god.

Have you ever shouted in a place with an echo and then heard your own words shouted back at you? In Greek mythology, Echo was a lovely nymph who died for love, leaving nothing behind but her voice. Astronomers have named the planets and many of the stars for the gods of mythology. The ancient Greeks believed that many of the *constellations*, or groups of stars, were gods or mythological animals. For example, the constellation Gemini was seen as the twin sons of the goddess Leda; Orion as a mighty hunter; and Pegasus as the magical winged horse. These names are still used for their color and imagery.

Myths have inspired many of the world's greatest poets, artists, musicians, and even scientists. They are among the most beautiful stories ever told. Mythology teaches us much about the way people of long ago thought and lived. Myths can be great fun to read.

For further information on:
Creatures of Mythology, *see* ANIMALS OF MYTH AND LEGEND, GORGON, MERMAID.
Gods, Goddesses, and Spirits, *see* CONSTELLATION, FATES, FURY, GENIE, GODS AND GODDESSES, MUSES.
How Myths Started, *see* MAGIC, RELIGION, SUPERSTITION.
Mythological People, *see* AMAZON, ANDROMEDA, DAEDALUS, HERCULES, PANDORA, PERSEUS, PROMETHEUS.
Related Articles, *see* DAY OF THE WEEK; FOLKLORE; GREECE, ANCIENT; LEGEND; MONTH; ROME, ANCIENT.

GREEK MYTHOLOGY

The following are some mythical characters that do not have separate articles in this encyclopedia. When there is a Roman equivalent for the Greek name, the character is listed under the Greek name, with the Roman in parentheses.

Ajax: Greek warrior; killed himself when Achilles' arms were awared to Odysseus.
Artemis (Diana): Twin sister of *Appollo*; goddess of the moon and a famous huntress.
Athene (Minerva): Goddess of wisdom and war, daughter of *Zeus* (Jupiter), chief of the gods. Athene sprang, fully grown and armed, from her father's head.
Dionysus (Bacchus): God of wine and fertile crops.
Hector: Son of Priam; chief hero of the Trojans; slain by Achilles.
Helen of Troy: Fairest woman in the world; cause of Trojan War.
Heracles (Hercules): Strongman who performed 12 labors to be free from bondage.
Odysseus (Ulysses): Greek hero of Trojan War; king of Ithaca; roamed for ten years after war.

The ancient Egyptians believed that their gods could come to Earth and enter anything they chose— a man, a statue, or a plant. They could answer questions through the creature or object they were in. So it became the custom to keep a sacred animal at the shrine of each god. At certain times the animal was asked questions about the future and the animal could answer "yes" or "no" by, for example, eating from one of two food troughs.

One of the reasons why Hernando Cortés was able to conquer the Aztecs of Mexico in the 16th century was because the Aztecs believed in a mythological god named Quetzalcoatl. The god, who had a white skin and a beard, disappeared on a journey eastward. But he told the Aztecs that he would one day return in the form of a man. The Aztecs, seeing the white-skinned and bearded Cortés, thought he was Quetzalcoatl returning and welcomed him with honor. Cortés, of course, did nothing to stop the idea as it made his conquest much easier.

NAME A person is distinctively known or identified by his or her name. Names help us remember who different people are and to which families they belong.

Most of the names we use today once had special meanings in the languages from which they came. *David*, a popular name for boys, means "beloved." *Barbara* means "stranger." *Mary* means "bitter," and *Susan* means "lily." *Michael* means "godlike," and *Steven* means "crown." *Jennifer* means "white wave."

Parents usually choose the names for their children. Sometimes they choose a particular name because it has a nice sound or because it was the name of a favorite relative or a famous person.

Most people in Western countries today have a first name, middle name, and last name. The first name is also called a *given name*. The second name, or *middle name*, may be simply another name that the parents like, or it may be an old family name. Sometimes it is the mother's *maiden name*,

her last name before she married. The last name, or *surname*, is the same for all the children of one family who have the same mother and father. Sometimes fathers give their sons the very same names as their own, adding "junior" (Jr.) at the end to show that he is the son, not the father.

Hundreds of years ago, people often received their names from the places they lived, the type of work they did, or some personal characteristic. A man who lived by a hill might be called Mr. *Hill*. If he lived on the west side of the village, he might be called Mr. *West*. The village baker's last name became *Baker*, and this is the way names such as *Miller*, *Taylor*, and *Bowman* (an archer) came into existence. *Smith*, the most common last name in the United States, is a shortened form of blacksmith. If a man whose name was Jack or John had a son, the son was often called *Jackson* or *Johnson*, meaning "Jack's son" or "John's son." Sometimes these names omitted the word "son." For example, the name *Roberts* simply meant "Robert's (son)." People with some outstanding personal characteristic, such as strength or height, sometimes took that quality as their surname, forming names such as *Strong* and *Long*.

In Scotland and Ireland, surnames were often formed by adding a prefix to the father's name. The Irish prefixes "Mc" and "O" were added to form such names as *O'Brien* (grandson of Brien) and *McConnell* (son of Connell). The Scottish "Mac" formed such names as *MacDonald* (son of Donald). Russian middle names are formed by adding "ovich" (for males) or "ovna" (for females) to the father's given name. For example, *Ivanovich* means "son of Ivan." *Petrovna* means "daughter of Peter."

Many people have nicknames made by shortening their first names. A boy named Michael may be called "Mike." Some people are given nicknames because of special ways they look or behave. For example, a person with red hair may be called "Red."

Some names have come to be considered masculine or feminine. Names such as David and William are considered masculine because they have always been given to boys. Names such as Anne and Kathleen are considered feminine because they have always been given to girls. Other names, such as Leslie, Dale, and Meredith can be given to children of either sex.

Actors and actresses may have *stage* *names* by which they are known in the theater. Writers may publish books under a different name, called a *pseudonym* or *pen name*. Criminals sometimes go by another name, or *alias*, so they will not be discovered. Famous people who want to travel without being recognized go *incognito*, which means that they use a different name for a while. But most people keep the same names all their lives.

NAMIBIA Namibia is in the southwest part of Africa. Many maps show this country as "South West Africa." It is bounded on the north by Angola, by Botswana on the east, and by South Africa on the southeast and south. Namibia's long west coast lies along the Atlantic Ocean. Windhoek is the capital. (See the map with the article on AFRICA.)

The bleak Namib Desert follows the Atlantic shoreline. Most of the country is a plateau averaging 3,600 feet (1,100 m) in height. In the east lies a part of the Kalahari Desert. There is not much good farmland in Namibia. The main industry is mining. Namibia is one of the world's largest producers of diamonds. Fishing and raising livestock are also important.

Bushmen live in the Kalahari on what they hunt and what little plant food they can gather. Ancient carvings and paintings on rocks done by the Bushmen tell something about the

The most common surname in the world is Chang. It has been estimated that there are at least 80 million Chinese named Chang.

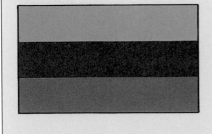

NAMIBIA

Capital City: Windhoek (115,000 people).
Area: 318,261 square miles (824,232 sq. km).
Population: 1,480,000.
Government: Ruled by South Africa.
Natural Resources: Diamonds, copper, zinc, uranium, tin, vanadium, natural gas.
Export Products: Diamonds, uranium, copper, zinc, meat, processed fish, karakel skins.
Unit of Money: Rand.
Official Languages: Afrikaans, English.

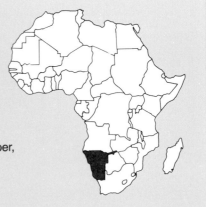

▲ *A church in Windhoek, the capital of Namibia.*

African forces in 1915. South West Africa then became a South African territory under a mandate from the League of Nations. In 1946, the United Nations (which replaced the League) rejected South Africa's application to take over the territory. South Africa argued that the U.N. had no rights over Namibia and ruled it as part of South Africa. The South West African People's Organization opposed South African control and began a guerilla war in 1966. In 1989, South Africa handed over power, and after free elections Namibia became independent in 1990.

ALSO READ: AFRICA, SOUTH AFRICA.

NANSEN, FRIDTJOF see EXPLORATION, OCEAN.

NAPOLEON BONAPARTE (1769-1821) Napoleon Bonaparte was one

▼ *Napoleon invaded Russia in June 1812 with about 600,000 men. The bitter Russian winter and lack of supplies forced him to retreat, and many of his soldiers died on the long march home.*

way of life many thousands of years ago. The Bushmen and Hottentots speak Xhoison, or "click," languages. These languages are unusual due to the clicking sounds that speakers produce in the throat to form the words that are used. Other groups speak Bantu. About nine percent of the population is of European descent.

The Portuguese explorer, Bartholomeu Dias, discovered the area in the 1400's. It was later colonized by German immigrants in the 1800's and then invaded and captured by South

of the most brilliant military leaders of all time. He was born on the Mediterranean island of Corsica and was trained to be a soldier from an early age. When he was 19 years old, the French Revolution began. Napoleon joined the revolutionary armies in France, fighting against the French king. He was wounded in battle several times and received many military honors.

Napoleon was made a brigadier general in the French army when he was only 24 years old. At that time, the revolutionary government in France (called the "Directory") was at war with Austria and Prussia. The Directory put Napoleon in command of French forces fighting against the Austrians in Italy in 1796. He led the French troops to victory in a series of great battles.

Napoleon returned to Paris, a hero of the French people. He helped overthrow the Directory in 1799 and set up a new government called the "Consulate," with himself as head. Napoleon made many changes in France. He established a new school system and modernized French law. The Napoleonic Code, as the unified body of French law is called, became the model for many legal systems.

On December 2, 1804, Napoleon had himself crowned emperor of France. He then wanted an heir to succeed him. His marriage to the beautiful Joséphine de Beauharnais had been childless. Napoleon divorced her in 1809 and married Princess Marie Louise, the daughter of the emperor of Austria, in 1810. She bore him a son, who was given the title Napoleon II.

In a series of brilliant military campaigns, French armies under Napoleon conquered almost all of the European continent. In 1812, Napoleon set out to invade Russia with more than 600,000 soldiers, the largest army ever formed in Europe. As the Russian army retreated, they destroyed all the food they could find in the countryside, so the French forces would have nothing to eat. The Russians knew that winter was coming and the weather would soon be very cold. When Napoleon reached Moscow, the capital of Russia, the snow had begun to fall. Napoleon found Moscow in flames and almost empty. His troops, finding no shelter or food, were forced to begin the terrible journey home in the freezing

▲ *Napoleon Bonaparte, a master of strategy, made use of his brilliant sense of timing to gain victory on the battlefield.*

Napoleon was not very tall and was known affectionately as "the little corporal" by his soldiers.

▲ *Napoleon's first wife was the Empress Josephine. Her failure to produce an heir led to divorce, but when Napoleon was on his deathbed in St. Helena, her name was one of the last words he uttered.*

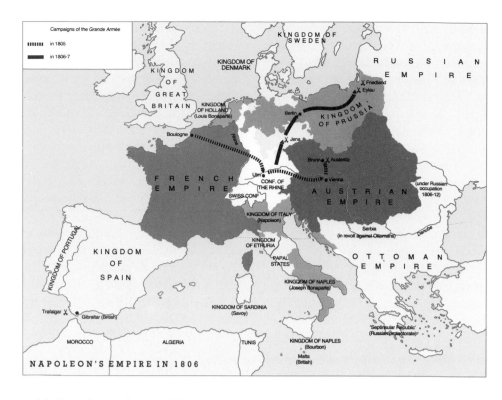

NAPOLEON'S EMPIRE IN 1806

During Napoleon's reign in France, women's hair fashions became very ornamental. The ornaments included flowers, fruit, jewels, and even model carriages and ships. These headdresses were often so tall that the wearer had to go down on her knees to get in and out of coach doors.

▼ *Napoleon (seated) on the island of St. Helena where he was exiled by the British in October 1815.*

cold Russian winter. Fewer than 100,000 of them reached France.

With Napoleon's armies so weakened, Great Britain, Prussia, Austria, Sweden, and Russia formed an alliance against France. Napoleon was defeated at the Battle of Leipzig in 1813, and the allies took Paris the following year. Napoleon gave up his throne and was exiled to the island of Elba, off the coast of Italy.

Napoleon escaped from Elba in 1815 and returned to France. He was welcomed enthusiastically by the French people. For a short period known as the "Hundred Days," Napoleon again became France's leader. He quickly gathered a new army, and France's enemies again declared war. Napoleon was defeated at the great battle of Waterloo by the British and Prussian armies. Napoleon escaped capture but later gave himself up to the British. This time he was sent to the desolate island of St. Helena, located in the Atlantic Ocean midway between Africa and South America. Napoleon died there six years later. He was buried on the island, but his body was taken to Paris in 1840 to be entombed in the Hôtel des Invalides,

a hospital for disabled soldiers that is now a military museum.

ALSO READ: EUROPE, FRENCH HISTORY, FRENCH REVOLUTION, HOLY ROMAN EMPIRE, WATERLOO.

NARCOTICS Narcotics are drugs that dull the senses (thus reducing pain) and cause sleep. For these reasons, narcotics have been used for centuries by doctors as medicines. But narcotics also become *addictive* when used for a long time—they create in the user a physical need for the drug. The use of narcotics without a doctor's prescription is illegal. Some narcotics, such as opium and heroin, are so dangerous that doctors are no longer allowed to prescribe them.

Many people use narcotics just to get "high" (in good spirits). After the habit has been established, larger doses of the drugs must be used to get the same effect. The victim's body develops a need for the drug and cannot function properly without it. He or she is then a drug addict.

Other drugs can become addictive, too. Drugs called *amphetamines* are stimulants, often prescribed by doctors as a temporary means of overcoming tiredness. But some people abuse these drugs and take amphetamines just to get "high," to feel alert and happy for a little while.

Drugs called *barbiturates* are sedatives. They are often prescribed by doctors to help patients relax or sleep. Taken in high doses, however, barbiturates produce effects like those of alcoholic drunkenness. Later, the user may fall into a deep sleep. Barbiturate overdoses are a major cause of poison deaths in the United States.

Opium is a narcotic made from the juice of the opium poppy. Opium is used to make other narcotics, including *morphine*, *paregoric*, and *codeine*. *Heroin* is actually morphine that has been treated with chemicals to make it about four times stronger. Morphine is occasionally prescribed as medicine, but heroin is too addictive for safe medical use. *Meperidine* (Demerol) and *codeine*, which are sometimes used in cough syrups, are milder narcotics, but they can also become addictive when they are used for a long time.

Cocaine is a drug made from the leaves of the South American coca plant. It stimulates the nervous system, and is not prescribed by doctors. Cocaine is an addictive narcotic, and it is illegal to use or sell it. *Crack* is a powerful drug made from cocaine. Crack is very dangerous. Like heroin, it can kill. It is very easy to become addicted to crack, and it is illegal to use it.

Narcotic drugs, such as morphine and heroin, affect many parts of the body, especially the brain. They make the user's senses much less sharp, less aware of the world around him or her. In doing this, the narcotics kill feelings of hunger and thirst, so most drug addicts do not eat and drink properly. They lose weight and lose resistance to bacteria that cause disease. Drug addicts are more likely than other people to get pneumonia, tuberculosis, and other diseases.

Persons convicted of illegally buying or selling narcotics are usually sent to prison. Addicts must receive medical and psychiatric treatment to break their drug habit. The Federal Government operates hospitals in Fort Worth, Texas, and Lexington, Kentucky, to treat addicts. Drug addiction has become so widespread in recent years that other programs have been started to help addicts. Almost every state in the United States has set up programs to help addicts. Narcotics Anonymous and other organizations made up of former addicts try to help addicts break the drug habit. Some programs treat addicts with *methadone*, an artificial drug that relieves an addict's physical need for more dangerous narcotics.

ALSO READ: ADDICTION, DRUG, DRUG ABUSE.

▲ *Opium is obtained from the seed pod of the opium poppy.*

NASSER, GAMAL ABDEL (1918–1970) Gamal Abdel Nasser, an Egyptian army officer, was the first president of the Arab Republic of Egypt. His efforts to gain a better life for Egyptians and to unify the Arab nations made him a hero to many Arabs.

Nasser was born in Ben Mor, Egypt. He graduated from the Royal Military Academy of Egypt in 1938 and became an instructor at the Army Staff College four years later. He fought in the Arab war against Israel in 1948. As a lieutenant colonel, he led a group of officers who overthrew King Farouk and established Egypt as a republic in 1952. Nasser became deputy premier and minister of the interior. He forced the premier from office in 1954 and became premier himself. Nasser was elected president in 1956.

As president, Nasser took land from the wealthy landlords and gave it to poor farmers. He also brought the Suez Canal under Egyptian control. This led to a brief war with Great Britain and France in 1956. The United Nations stopped the war. When Egypt and Syria joined together to form the United Arab Re-

Opium as a drug has been known for a very long time. Homer, the ancient Greek poet, describes tea made from it. But smoking opium did not start until well after the discovery of America. Smoking of any kind was unknown in the Old World until tobacco was introduced from America.

▲ *Gamal Abdel Nasser, a great Egyptian leader.*

▼ *The delegation of Bhutan seated at the United Nations General Assembly in New York City. The tiny kingdom of Bhutan, located in the Himalaya Mountains of Asia, was admitted to the family of nations in 1971.*

public in 1958, Nasser was elected the first president of the republic. He led the Arab nations in the Six-Day War against Israel in 1967 and offered to resign as president when the Arabs were defeated. The Egyptian people insisted he remain in office. Three years later, he died of a heart attack.

ALSO READ: EGYPT, ISRAEL, MIDDLE EAST, SUEZ CANAL, SYRIA.

NATION The word "nation" comes from the Latin word meaning "to be born." From Biblical times, "nation" referred to a group of people who were born at the same place. During the 1600's, the word "nation" gradually came to mean any *sovereign state* (a country that is completely independent). For example, the state of New York is not sovereign because it is part of the United States and owes its allegiance (loyalty) to the United States. In the 1700's, the word "nation" came to refer to all the people who live under the government of a sovereign state.

A nation may be very tiny or very large. Liechtenstein is smaller in area than Washington, D.C., and has fewer than 27,000 citizens. The People's Republic of China is larger than the United States and has a population of more than one billion citizens. A nation may be based on democracy, socialism, fascism, monarchism, or any other political system. A nation may be ruled by an elected president

and legislature or a dictator. But all nations are independent and self-governing.

How does a group of people become a nation? Certain things tend to unite people. The most important of these is a common language. Also important are a common religion, a common ancestry, and shared traditions. Sometimes a common enemy causes people to unite. Geography can also affect the development of a nation—but there are exceptions. The Pyrenees (a mountain range) divide the nations of France and Spain. But the people on both sides of the Nile River need the water of the Nile to irrigate their land and to travel on. The Nile has united the people of Egypt. There are exceptions to the other characteristics, too. Canada has two official languages. The United States is made up of people of many different races and cultural backgrounds.

Citizens usually feel a certain amount of love for and loyalty to their nation. This feeling, called *patriotism*, is often what links people together in a common effort to build their nation and defend it. When the citizens of a nation feel that their nation is more important than any other nation, it is called *nationalism*. The extreme nationalism of many Germans who believed that Germany was better than any other nation was a major cause of World War II. But it was also a feeling of nationalism that inspired many colonies to win their independence from the countries that governed them. This is particularly true of the many new African nations that have recently won their independence.

For further information on:
Development of Nations, *see* CIVILIZATION, COMMUNITY, CULTURE, CUSTOMS, HUMAN BEINGS.
Establishment of Nations, *see* ARTICLES OF CONFEDERATION, BILL OF RIGHTS, CITIZENSHIP, COLONY, CONTI-

NENTAL CONGRESS, DECLARATION OF INDEPENDENCE, FATHERS OF CONFEDERATION, GOVERNMENT, IMMIGRATION, REVOLUTION.

Natural Boundaries Between Nations, *see* ALPS MOUNTAINS, ANDES MOUNTAINS, ENGLISH CHANNEL, RED SEA, RIO GRANDE.

Organizations of Nations, *see* COMMONWEALTH OF NATIONS, ECONOMIC EUROPEAN COMMUNITY, LEAGUE OF NATIONS, NORTH ATLANTIC TREATY ORGANIZATION, ORGANIZATION OF AMERICAN STATES, UNITED NATIONS, WARSAW PACT.

Relations Among Nations, *see* INTERNATIONAL LAW, INTERNATIONAL RELATIONS, INTERNATIONAL TRADE, TREATY, WAR.

For individual nations see Index at name.

NATIONAL ANTHEM People all over the world sing when they feel happy or glad. The word *anthem* means "a song of praise or gladness," a kind of hymn. When people need a song to express how they feel about their country they call it a national anthem. *The Star-Spangled Banner* is the national anthem of the United States.

Anthems used to be sung in praise of God instead of country. After the Middle Ages, people thought of themselves as belonging more to nations instead of to city-states or small principalities, so they created anthems in praise of their nations.

France's national anthem, *La Marseillaise*, is called the *Hymne Nationale*. Written by Rouget de Lisle, it was sung in 1792 by soldiers from Marseille during the French Revolution. Translated, it begins:

Go forward, children of the
    fatherland,
The Day of Glory has arrived!
Many national anthems were written in times of national crisis and were first adopted by the armed forces.

The music for some national anthems was written by famous composers. The West German national anthem, *Deutschland Über Alles* ("Germany Above All"), was composed by Franz Joseph Haydn. The Finnish national anthem, *Finlandia*, was composed by Jean Sibelius. The music for *O Canada* was taken from an opera entitled *The Magic Flute* by Wolfgang Amadeus Mozart.

In the British national anthem as sung today, the word "queen" appears in the first two lines:

God save our gracious Queen,
Long live our noble Queen.
The word is changed to "king" when the monarch is a king. The song dates back to the middle 1700's. Manuscripts from that date show that an organist by the name of John Bull wrote the song.

The Russians have had three different national anthems during the twentieth century. *God Preserve Our Czar* was changed after the Russian Revolution to the *Internationale*, and then changed again in the 1940's to *Unbreakable Union of Freeborn Republics.*

Japan's national anthem is the oldest, with ancient words dating from the A.D. 800's. Greece has the longest with 158 verses, and Japan, Jordan, and San Marino have the shortest anthems—only four lines.

ALSO READ: STAR-SPANGLED BANNER.

NATIONAL ASSOCIATION FOR THE ADVANCEMENT OF COLORED PEOPLE Better known as the NAACP, the National Association for the Advancement of Colored People is a civil rights organization that works for the rights of blacks and other minority groups. About 500,000 men and women of all races are NAACP members.

The NAACP was founded on February 12, 1909 (the one-hundredth anniversary of Abraham Lincoln's

▲ *France's stirring national anthem*, La Marseillaise, *was born out of the turmoil of the French Revolution.*

The Star-Spangled Banner did not officially become the United States national anthem until March 3, 1931, when an Act of Congress was passed to that effect. The full anthem has four verses.

▲ *American civil rights leaders in 1964, shown with Roy Wilkins (center), then head of the NAACP. They include Dr. Martin Luther King, Jr. (fourth from right), Whitney M. Young, Jr. (third from left), and James Farmer (fourth from left).*

birth), by 60 black and white people who were concerned about the civil rights of blacks. After two blacks were lynched during racial riots in Springfield, Illinois, a white social worker named Mary White Ovington organized a meeting of citizens interested in working for equality for blacks. The NAACP developed from this meeting.

Through the years, the NAACP has tried to improve conditions for blacks and others through *litigation* (taking cases to court), *legislation* (getting civil rights laws passed in Congress and in state legislatures), and *education* (informing people about the need of equality for everyone). The NAACP does this by supporting blacks and others in court, by promoting the passage of civil rights laws, and by informing people of their rights as American citizens. In 1954, NAACP lawyers took a case (*Brown v. the Board of Education of Topeka, Kansas*) involving school segregation to the Supreme Court. The Court ruled that segregation in public schools is unconstitutional. This decision made it possible to spotlight unconstitutional inequalities in other aspects of life besides the schools. The NAACP magazine, *Crisis*, is published monthly to keep the members informed about NAACP activities.

The NAACP has more that 1,700 branches in the United States. Their activities depend largely on local problems. Some groups have organized boycotts or "selective buying" activities to discourage stores from treating black employees and customers unfairly. Some have picketed businesses and organizations that discriminate against people. Others have joined together for marches or sit-ins. Many groups encourage and help black citizens to register to vote. The NAACP's Washington office makes certain the interests of black people are represented in Congress and keeps in contact with government agencies.

The NAACP was headed by Walter Francis White from 1931 to 1955 and by Roy Wilkins from 1955 to 1977. Today, Benjamin L. Hooks is the NAACP executive director.

ALSO READ: BLACK AMERICANS, CIVIL RIGHTS, CIVIL RIGHTS MOVEMENT.

NATIONAL FOREST Would you like to see some of the tallest and oldest trees in the world? Or visit a tropical rain forest? Maybe you would enjoy seeing a colony of beavers at work. These are just a few of the wonders that attract more than 100 million visitors to the nation's 155 national forests each year.

The national forests are areas of land owned by the people of the United States and managed by the Forest Service of the U.S. Department of Agriculture. They are located throughout the United States and in Puerto Rico. The national forests serve many useful purposes. They provide recreation areas for the public. You can camp, swim, and hike in most of these areas free of charge. You can also go fishing, boating, and skiing in some forests. Other forests are set aside as wilderness areas. These areas provide homes for the nation's wildlife—both plants and animals. No trees can be cut down in wilderness areas, nor buildings built there. Some national forests are not really forests at all. They are grasslands with grazing for animals.

You may think that national forests sound very much like national parks. But they differ in one very important way. National forests make money for the government and for private companies. Lumber companies pay the government for the right to cut down full-grown trees. Mining companies also pay a fee for the right to take ore from forest lands. Cattle companies pay the government a fee so that their herds may graze on the grasslands. The money made by these activities (none of which is permitted in the national parks) helps maintain the forests.

The people responsible for protecting the resources of the forests are called *forest rangers*. Rangers make sure no timber or minerals are taken from the forest illegally, and no animals are permitted to graze unless their owners have paid for permits. They protect the trees from fires, insects, and diseases. They plant seedlings to replace those trees removed by lumber companies. Forest rangers also keep up the public campgrounds and enforce hunting and fishing regulations.

▲ *These ancient giant Redwood trees in the Six Rivers National Forest, California, literally dwarf this passing camper.*

The first forest preserves were established in the western states during the 1890's. They were officially named national forests and put under the control of the Forest Service in 1905. Gifford Pinchot, one of America's first great conservationists, became the first chief of the Forest Service. He helped develop the system for operating the forests.

ALSO READ: CAMPING, CONSERVATION, FOREST FIRE, FORESTRY, LUMBER AND LUMBERING, NATIONAL PARK, NATURAL RESOURCES.

▼ *National forests include land for animal grazing, as well as wilderness areas with scenic mountains and lakes. Visitors to national forests can go hiking, fishing and canoeing.*

NATIONAL GUARD The National Guard consists of units (groups) of voluntary, part-time soldiers from each of the states, Puerto Rico, and the District of Columbia. The National Guard has two branches—the Army National Guard and the Air National Guard.

The National Guard began in colonial times as the *militia*, groups of civilian volunteers trained to deal with local emergencies. After the American Revolution, the Constitution provided for the continuation of the militia. In 1824, the New York State Militia named itself the National Guard. By the beginning of the 1900's, most of the states had followed New York's example.

Each state or regional government recruits volunteers for its National

The national forests of the United States cover an area of nearly 200 million acres, larger than all of California and Oregon.

▲ *The National Guard was called in to restore order during riots in Chicago following the assassination of Martin Luther King, Jr. in 1968.*

▼ *The Statue of Liberty, a national monument, celebrated her 100th birthday in July 1986 after restoration that took two years and cost 70 million dollars.*

Guard units and provides part of the money needed to support them. Each governor is commander-in-chief of the state's National Guard units. The Federal Government provides the equipment for the Guard, supervises the training of volunteers, and provides most of the financial support.

The National Guard serves in either national or local emergencies. National Guard units can be called into active duty by a Presidential order. The President may order National Guard units into active service during war or some other national emergency, such as a rebellion against federal authorities. When National Guard units are called into federal service, they become part of the Army or Air Force. The governor of a state may call to duty National Guard units for a local emergency—any situation considered dangerous to public safety, life, or property. These situations may be natural emergencies, such as floods, or man-made, such as riots.

Volunteers for the National Guard must meet the same physical, mental, and educational requirements as members of the regular Army or Air Force. Members of the Guard must train for a weekend each month. Members must also take part in two weeks of field training every summer at a military camp. Guard members are given a *pension* (retirement pay) when their service is ended. Persons

who will be called into the regular army are usually allowed to volunteer for the National Guard as a substitute military service.

ALSO READ: AIR FORCE, ARMY.

NATIONAL MONUMENT National monuments are government lands in the United States that have been set aside as protected places for all people to enjoy. They contain priceless natural landmarks or areas of scientific, historic, or prehistoric interest.

These publicly owned monuments, along with national parks, memorials, and other national historical and military parks and sites, are run by the National Park Service of the Department of the Interior. The National Park Service was established by Congress in 1916.

The Antiquities Act, passed by Congress on June 8, 1906, gave the President authority to establish national monuments. The first was Devils Tower, an 865-foot (264-m) tower of volcanic rock in Wyoming.

Today, the government has set aside 91 national monuments on about 10 million acres (4 million hectares) of federally owned land. These monuments include such attractions as a lava flow hardening into the basalt columns of the Devils Postpile in California; Fossil Butte in Wyoming, where fish fossils are more than 40 million years old; Custer Battlefield in Montana, where the historic battle with the Sioux Indians was fought; the Statue of Liberty in New York Harbor, which has become a great symbol of freedom; Rainbow Bridge in Utah, the world's largest known natural bridge—309 feet (94 m) high and 278 feet (85 m) long; and Yucca House in Colorado, which is the ruin of a large ancient Indian pueblo.

ALSO READ: NATIONAL FOREST, NATIONAL PARK.

NATIONAL PARK Large tracts of public lands in the United States and in other countries of the world are preserved for all the people as national parks. These lands contain much of a country's most spectacular natural scenery, such as glaciers, canyons, and mountain peaks.

Congress sets aside land for the U.S. parks and decides on their boundaries. Hunting is forbidden and fishing is regulated in the parks, in order to protect wildlife. A superintendent is responsible for each national park, and park rangers and guides help people explore and enjoy the areas. National parks also employ naturalists, foresters, biologists, geologists, and historians to study the park areas and find out how the formations developed.

The idea of preserving natural land areas came about in 1870. A group of people on an expedition in Wyoming sat around a campfire one night. They talked of the thundering waterfalls, the forests, and great canyons and geysers of this land. They decided that the land should be protected as a park for people to enjoy in the future.

On March 1, 1872, President Grant signed a bill to create Yellowstone National Park, the first national park in the world. It was created as a public park for the benefit and enjoyment of all the people. Yellowstone is located in northwestern Wyoming and extends into Montana and Idaho.

In 1890, Congress voted to create more national parks, including Sequoia and Yosemite in California. Today, national parks are found in many states.

In 1916, Congress established the National Park Service within the Department of the Interior to "conserve the scenery and the natural and historic objects and wildlife." The National Park Service provides outdoor recreation, such as camping, boating, waterskiing, swimming, fishing, hiking, and bicycling. More than 200

million people visit the park service areas every year.

In 1933, Congress gave responsibility to the National Park Service to care for all national parks and monuments. In addition to the 40 national parks, the park system includes other parklike areas. For example, there are 22 national *historical parks*, such as Harper's Ferry, West Virginia. There are 91 national monuments, including the 2 million acres (809,400 hectares) of Death Valley, California, and the more than 2½ million acres (1,000,000 hectares) at Glacier Bay in Alaska. Of 24 national *memorials*, one of the most famous is the Mount Rushmore National Memorial in the Black Hills of South Dakota. There are also 10 national *battlefields*, 3 national *battlefield parks*, 10 national *military parks*, and 62 *historic sites*. One historic place is the John Fitzgerald Kennedy National Historical Site in Brookline, Massachusetts, birthplace of President John F. Kennedy.

More and more places of national historic interest are being considered for preservation under the Historic Sites Act of 1935. The National Park Service works with state and local government agencies to decide which locations and buildings should be preserved.

About one-third of the land in the

▲ *Some of the largest caves in the world can be seen in Carlsbad Caverns National Park in New Mexico. Tourists make their way through vast underground chambers adorned with gleaming stalactites and stalagmites.*

▼ *Old Faithful spouts its hot, steamy plumes of water over 100 feet (30 m) into the air. Thousands of tourists visit the hundreds of geysers in Yellowstone National Park.*

NATIONAL PARKS OF THE UNITED STATES

Name	Location	Area in acres	Area in hectares	Interesting features
Acadia	Maine	38,632	15,634	Spectacular wave-battered cliffs, interesting caves, beautiful lakes.
Arches	Utah	73,379	29,696	Unusual stone arches, windows, pinnacles, and pedestals caused by erosion.
Badlands	South Dakota	243,302	98,464	Dry area with deep ravines, colorful rocks, fossils
Big Bend	Texas	708,118	286,575	Wild animals, Rocky Mountains, Rio Grande.
Biscayne	Florida	173,274	70,124	Chain of islands south of Miami.
Bryce Canyon	Utah	38,835	15,717	14 box canyons, magnificent sheer curves of the Pink Cliffs.
Canyonlands	Utah	377,570	152,803	Huge mesas, strange rock formations, evidence of prehistoric Indians.
Capital Reef	Utah	241,904	97,899	Sixty-mile (97-km) elevation of sandstone cliffs, highly colored rock, narrow and high gorges.
Carlsbad Caverns	New Mexico	46,753	18,921	Fantastic labyrinth under the Guadalupe Mountains.
Channel Islands	California	124,740	50,482	Sea birds, sea lions, endangered wildlife.
Crater Lake	Oregon	160,290	64,869	An extinct volcano, Wizard Island, the Phantom Ship.
Denali	Alaska	4,700,000	1,900,000	Name changed from Mt. McKinley National Park—contains highest mountain in the United States.
Everglades	Florida	1,398,800	566,094	Mangrove and cypress swamps, rare birds.
Gates of the Arctic	Alaska	7,500,000	3,035,250	Vast north-central wilderness.
Glacier	Montana	1,013,595	410,202	60 glaciers and 250 lakes, Going-to-the-Sun Highway.
Glacier Bay	Alaska	3,225,198	1,305,238	Coastal glaciers that move down to the sea.
Grand Canyon	Arizona	1,218,375	493,076	Enormous canyon shaped by the Colorado River.
Grand Teton	Wyoming	310,516	125,666	Breathtaking range of mountains, picturesque lakes.
Great Basin	Nevada	76,800	31,080	Deserts, high mountain peaks, bristle-cone pines.
Great Smoky Mountains	North Carolina and Tennessee	517,369	209,379	Mountains, forests, lakes, variety of wildlife.
Guadalupe Mountains	Texas	76,293	30,876	McKittrick Canyon open to the public, rest of park closed.
Haleakala	Hawaii (Mauri Island)	28,655	11,597	Great dormant volcano.
Hawaii Volcanoes	Hawaii (Hawaii Island)	229,177	92,748	Active volcanoes, awe-inspiring fire pit.
Hot Springs	Arkansas	5,826	2,358	47 hot mineral springs used to treat a number of sicknesses.
Isle Royale	Michigan	571,796	231,406	Wildlife preserve on a fascinating island in western Lake Superior.
Katmai	Alaska	3,716,000	1,503,865	Valley of Ten Thousand Smokes—volcanic activity.
Kenai Fjords	Alaska	670,000	271,149	Marine mammals, birdlife abundant.
Kings Canyon	California	460,136	186,217	Mountains, meadows, forests, lakes, streams, canyons.
Kobuk Valley	Alaska	1,750,000	708,208	River is center of the native culture.
Lake Clark	Alaska	2,874,000	1,163,079	Scenic wilderness across Cook Inlet from Anchorage.
Lassen Volcanic	California	106,372	43,049	Active volcanoes, boiling lakes, lava fields.
Mammoth Cave	Kentucky	52,452	21,227	Largest single cave in the world.
Mesa Verde	Colorado	52,085	21,079	Largest cliff dwellings and pueblos in North America.
Mount Rainier	Washington	235,404	95,268	Extinct volcano with glaciers spreading from its crater.
North Cascades	Washington	504,781	204,285	Mountains, glaciers, lakes.
Olympic	Washington	908,781	367,784	Mountains, giant evergreens, flower-drenched meadows, rain forest.
Petrified Forest	Arizona	93,493	37,837	Forest of petrified wood, prehistoric Indian dwellings.
Redwood	California	109,027	44,123	Groves of ancient redwood trees along Pacific Coast.
Rocky Mountain	Colorado	263,809	106,764	Rocky Mountains, lakes, streams, flowers.
Sequoia	California	403,023	163,103	Enormous sequoia trees, mountains.
Shenandoah	Virginia	194,826	78,846	Blue Ridge Mountains, spectacular scenery from Skyline Drive.
Theodore Roosevelt	North Dakota	70,416	28,497	Little Missouri River valley and T. Roosevelt's ranch.
Virgin Islands	Virgin Islands	14,695	5,947	Rich tropical vegetation, beaches of beautiful white sand.
Voyageurs	Minnesota	219,128	88,681	More than 50 lakes, large forests, wildlife.
Wind Cave	South Dakota	28,292	11,450	Large cavern, Black Hills.
Wrangell-St. Elias	Alaska	8,945,000	3,619,952	Largest area in park system.
Yellowstone	Wyoming, Montana, Idaho	2,219,823	898,362	Canyon, geysers, waterfalls, mountains, petrified forests.
Yosemite	California	760,917	307,943	Yosemite Valley in Sierra Nevada, waterfalls, beautiful scenery.
Zion	Utah	146,551	59,309	Canyons, cliffs.

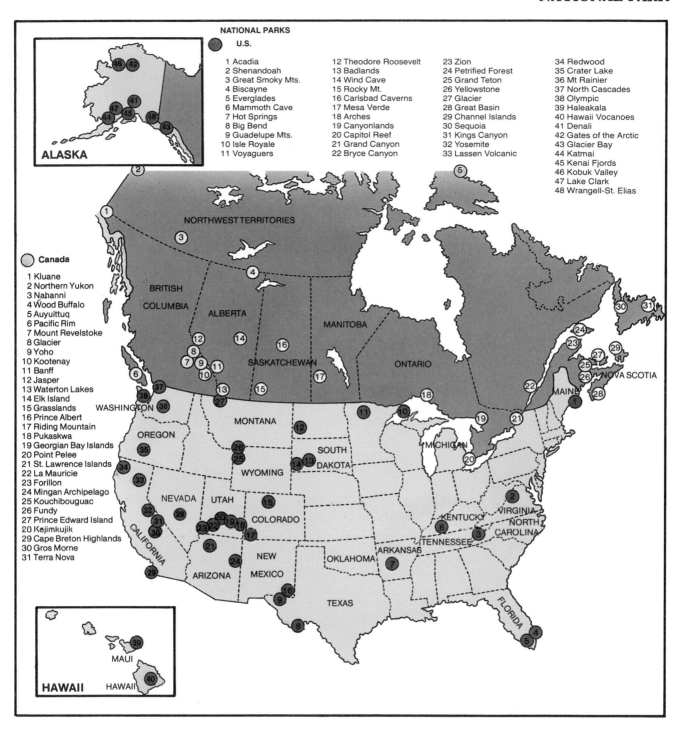

NATIONAL PARKS

U.S.

1 Acadia
2 Shenandoah
3 Great Smoky Mts.
4 Biscayne
5 Everglades
6 Mammoth Cave
7 Hot Springs
8 Big Bend
9 Guadelupe Mts.
10 Isle Royale
11 Voyaguers

12 Theodore Roosevelt
13 Badlands
14 Wind Cave
15 Rocky Mt.
16 Carlsbad Caverns
17 Mesa Verde
18 Arches
19 Canyonlands
20 Capitol Reef
21 Grand Canyon
22 Bryce Canyon

23 Zion
24 Petrified Forest
25 Grand Teton
26 Yellowstone
27 Glacier
28 Great Basin
29 Channel Islands
30 Sequoia
31 Kings Canyon
32 Yosemite
33 Lassen Volcanic

34 Redwood
35 Crater Lake
36 Mt Rainier
37 North Cascades
38 Olympic
39 Haleakala
40 Hawaii Vocanoes
41 Denali
42 Gates of the Arctic
43 Glacier Bay
44 Katmai
45 Kenai Fjords
46 Kobuk Valley
47 Lake Clark
48 Wrangell-St. Elias

Canada

1 Kluane
2 Northern Yukon
3 Nahanni
4 Wood Buffalo
5 Auyuittuq
6 Pacific Rim
7 Mount Revelstoke
8 Glacier
9 Yoho
10 Kootenay
11 Banff
12 Jasper
13 Waterton Lakes
14 Elk Island
15 Grasslands
16 Prince Albert
17 Riding Mountain
18 Pukaskwa
19 Georgian Bay Islands
20 Point Pelee
21 St. Lawrence Islands
22 La Mauricie
23 Forillon
24 Mingan Archipelago
25 Kouchibouguac
26 Fundy
27 Prince Edward Island
28 Kejimkujik
29 Cape Breton Highlands
30 Gros Morne
31 Terra Nova

United States is owned by the Federal Government. Much attention is being given to greater use of this land for recreation. Today, the United States has 17 national *recreational areas.* There are also four national *lakeshores,* 10 national *seashores,* 10 national scenic *rivers and riverways,* four national *parkways,* and one national scenic *trail* (the Appalachian Trail).

The restrictions in a recreational area are not so tight as those for a national park. For example, it might be possible for a privately owned company to get government permission to drill for oil in a "recreation area," but only if the drilling would not seriously interfere with the main purpose of the area, which is recreation. Oil drilling or similar commercial operations would not be allowed in a national park.

Kobuk Valley National Park in Alaska has surprising arctic sand dunes. These were formed thousands of years ago from shifting glacial deposits.

The National Park Service and other government agencies are interested in good conservation practices on federal lands. In 1966, the National Park Service set up three national planning centers for parks and recreation areas. These centers are run by landscape architects, ecologists, managers of natural resources, land planners, and engineers. All of these experts use their knowledge and skills to preserve the land and to make more and better places where families can rest, relax, and enjoy themselves

◄ *Visitors to Yellowstone National Park are observed by a black bear.*

NATIONAL PARKS OF CANADA

Name	Location	Area in acres	Area in hectares	Interesting features
Auyuittuq	Northwest Territories	5,305,600	2,147,176	Glaciers and fiords.
Banff	Alberta	1,640,960	664,097	Ice fields, hot springs, green valleys.
Cape Breton Highlands	Nova Scotia	234,880	95,056	Rugged mountains, green valleys.
Elk Island	Alberta	48,000	19,425	Fenced game preserve of buffalo, deer, elk, moose.
Forillon	Quebec	59,392	24,036	Scenic coast of Gaspé Peninsula.
Fundy	New Brunswick	50,880	20,591	Area of rich scenery, Bay of Fundy.
Georgian Bay Islands	Ontario	3,456	1,399	Ancient Chippewa Indian settlements, 30 islands.
Glacier	British Columbia	333,440	134,943	Snow-capped mountains, forests, glaciers, wild flowers.
Grasslands	Saskatchewan	34,559	140	Mixed-grass prairie, prairie dogs and antelope.
Gros Morne	Newfoundland	480,000	194,256	Waterfalls, fiord-like lakes, seacoast, mountains.
Jasper	Alberta	2,688,000	1,087,834	Mountains, lakes, forests, canyons.
Kejimkujik	Nova Scotia	92,800	37,556	Beautiful scenery, wilderness trails.
Kluane	Yukon Territory	5,440,000	2,201,568	Mountains, glaciers, Dall sheep.
Kootenay	British Columbia	347,520	140,641	Hot mineral springs, canyons, beautiful valleys.
Kouchibouguac	New Brunswick	55,680	22,534	Lagoons, bays, sandbars.
La Mauricie	Quebec	134,400	45,932	Mountains, woods, lakes.
Mingan Archipelago	Gulf of St. Lawrence	9,660,600	39,010	Area of about 40 islands, Atlantic puffins, rare plants and flowers.
Mount Revelstoke	British Columbia	64,400	25,901	Mountains, scenic highway.
Nahanni	Northwest Territories	1,177,600	476,575	Canyons, hot springs, waterfalls.
Northern Yukon	Yukon Territory	1,505,000	6,050	Migration route for Porcupine herd of barren-ground caribou, major waterfowl area.
Pacific Rim	British Columbia	96,000	38,851	Pacific seashore, beaches, sea lions.
Point Pelee	Ontario	3,840	1,554	Recreation area with good beaches.
Prince Albert	Saskatchewan	957,440	387,476	Lakes, forests, beaches.
Prince Edward Island	Prince Edward Island	4,480	1,813	Lakes and streams, forests.
Pukaskwa	Ontario	464,000	187,781	Rivers, lakes, wildlife.
Riding Mountain	Manitoba	734,720	297,341	Fascinating woodland and lake area.
St. Lawrence Islands	Ontario	1,024	414	Scenic islands on the St. Lawrence River.
Terra Nova	Newfoundland	99,840	40,405	Good fishing area with bays and lakes.
Waterton Lakes	Alberta	129,920	52,579	Waterfalls, lakes, interesting trails, rugged mountain peaks.
Wood Buffalo	Alberta and Northwest Territories	11,072,000	4,480,838	Home of greatest herd of buffalo in North America, whooping cranes.
Yoho	British Columbia	324,480	131,137	Waterfalls, lakes, beautiful Yoho Valley.

▲ *Mammoth Hot Springs near Gardiner, Montana, is a popular tourist attraction in Yellowstone National Park.*

in surroundings of natural beauty.

Canada's many beautiful national parks range from the mountains to the seacoasts. Mountains, ice fields, and lakes are found in Banff Park, which is located in western Alberta on the eastern slopes of the Canadian Rocky Mountains. The high peaks, canyons, and lakes of Jasper Park are nearby. Terra Nova is a seacoast park in eastern Newfoundland, and Fundy Park is on the Bay of Fundy in New Brunswick. Canada also has historic areas and two wild animal parks, Elk Island and Wood Buffalo.

■ **LEARN BY DOING**

Groups of children in several cities have worked with the National Park Service and other agencies to clean up vacant lots and make neighborhood recreational areas. Perhaps you and your friends could start such a project in your neighborhood. You won't be making a national park, but you would be helping your community. ■

ALSO READ: NATIONAL FOREST, NATIONAL MONUMENT, PARK.

NATURAL GAS A large amount of useful gas is trapped in rocks below the Earth's surface. This gas is called natural gas, to set it apart from gas that is made by scientists and other people. Natural gas consists mainly of *methane*, a chemical compound made up of the elements hydrogen and carbon (hydrocarbon).

Natural gas was probably formed from plants and animals that decayed millions of years ago. The decaying matter was buried beneath the Earth's surface, where it slowly changed into oil and gas. The rocks that hold natural gas are *porous*—full of pores, or tiny holes, which contain the gas. The gas is trapped and held underground in the porous rock by a covering of nonporous rock.

When shafts are drilled into the porous rock, the gas seeps out of the pores and into the shafts. Pipes are fitted into the shafts, and the gas can be brought to the surface to be used.

▲ *A glacier slides slowly down a valley between snowcapped mountains in Glacier National Park in Canada.*

▼ *The Yellowstone River flows through a wide valley in Yellowstone National Park.*

▲ *Farming in Tennessee. The soil in which food crops are grown is one of our most important natural resources.*

▼ *The map shows the main areas where petroleum, natural gas, and coal are mined, together with the chief areas where rivers are harnessed to produce hydroelectric power.*

The heavy hydrocarbons are taken out as liquids. The remaining dry gas is sent out through pipelines.

Natural gas is burned as fuel in industries and for heating homes and office buildings. It is also used for cooking. Natural gas has no odor, but an odor is always added, so that leaks can be noticed and traced.

Most natural gas in the United States comes from Texas, Oklahoma, California, Louisiana, and West Virginia. Natural gas is often found in ground that also contains petroleum. The supply of natural gas is diminishing as people use more and more of it.

ALSO READ: FUEL, GAS, NORTH SEA.

NATURALIZATION see CITIZENSHIP, IMMIGRATION.

NATURAL RESOURCES Natural resources are the riches provided by nature, such as water, soil, forests, wildlife, and minerals. Water is a major natural resource of all nations. Many scientists say that the air should also be considered a natural resource. Oxygen in the air is necessary for human and animal life, and carbon dioxide in the air is necessary for plant life.

There are two kinds of natural resources—resources that can be replaced or renewed (such as forests, grass, fish, and wildlife), and resources that cannot be replaced (such as coal and other minerals).

People have always tried to use the natural resources around them. Prehistoric people had to use natural resources just as they found them. They caught animals and picked plants with their hands. They used caves, overhanging rock, thick bushes, and tall trees for shelter and protection. From stones and minerals, people learned to make tools with which they could get more resources from nature. People's tools became more and more complicated—weapons, traps, fishing nets, fire, axes, needles. Besides eating animals, peo-

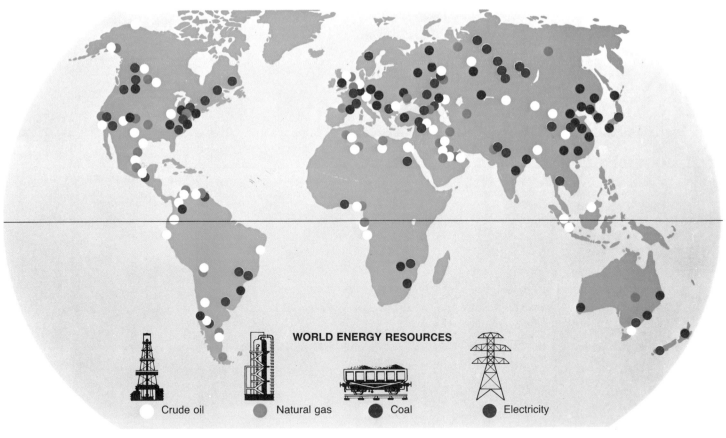

WORLD ENERGY RESOURCES

Crude oil   Natural gas   Coal   Electricity

ple used animal bones for tools and hides for clothing.

About 12,000 years ago, people began to change nature as they used natural resources. They tamed animals and learned how to plant and grow crops. They learned to control their own food resources. As time went on, they built artificial waterways (canals and irrigation streams) to control the flow of water. They dug mines to bring valuable copper, tin, lead, and other metals to the surface. They built boats and traveled out to take large fish and other resources from the ocean. They sailed to distant lands where they discovered new resources.

In the American colonies, people cut down forests, planted crops on vast areas of land, and built cities. The Industrial Revolution increased the number and amount of resources people could use. New machines needed fuel—first coal and oil, then electricity, and now atomic energy. Modern industrial machinery and the greatly increased population have used up natural resources at a very fast rate. People are now beginning to realize that unless they control their use of natural resources, many resources will disappear before nature can replace them.

Natural resources give strength to a nation. Some countries, such as the United States, the Soviet Union, and Canada, have great quantities of natural resources that they have used extensively. Some countries with a lot of natural resources have not had the tools to use them. These nations are called "underdeveloped." An underdeveloped nation must locate the resources it has and then build or obtain the machines and factories with which to make use of the resources. Nations that have only a few natural resources must develop those that they have and then trade with other countries.

Since World War II, people have been using natural resources at such a

fast rate that they have created some serious problems in their environment. For example, harmful chemicals, smoke, and other waste products created by manufacturing are poured into the lakes and rivers, blown into the air, or buried in the soil. The waste from homes, offices, and stores has made many rivers and streams as polluted as open sewers. *Pesticides* are used to kill insects harmful to food crops, but they also poison wildlife. Bulldozers and giant electric saws tear up grasslands and forests. Great highways change the landscape, upsetting plant and animal life. Millions of automobiles on these highways poison the air with dangerous fumes and smoke. In some cities, *smog* (air that is heavily polluted with fumes and smoke) has already brought death to some people and serious lung ailments to others. Smog also kills trees and plants.

People are finally becoming aware that natural resources are in real danger, which means that people's health and life are also in danger. Federal, state, and local governments have passed laws to control waste disposal, industrial smoke, automobile exhausts, and other causes of air and

▲ *Mining sands in Australia. Both quarrying and mining are fairly common along the shore.*

▲ *Grasshoppers, caterpillars, and other insects in the grass can be collected with a sturdy net called a sweep net. Sweep the net from side to side through the vegetation in front of you and then examine it. You will find lots of spiders and small flies in the net. Use a lens to have a close look at them.*

water pollution. Each person must do what he or she can to help save natural resources and make the world a healthy place in which to live.

ALSO READ: AIR, AIR POLLUTION, CONSERVATION, ECOLOGY, INDUSTRIAL REVOLUTION, LUMBER AND LUMBERING, MINERAL, MINES AND MINING, SOIL, WATER, WATER POLLUTION.

NATURAL SELECTION see EVOLUTION.

NATURE STUDY Nature study means learning about nature by observing plants, animals, rocks, the weather, the stars and planets—everything around us in nature. It is best to study plants and animals in their natural environment (surroundings) whenever possible. Parks and national forests usually have nature trails, where names of plants and animals and information about them are given. Or you and your friends may take a nature walk through a park, meadow, or wooded area near your home. Science classes often go on nature walks as field trips. You may want to take some things, such as rocks, leaves, or dead insects home with you to study more closely. But try not to disturb living things or their homes when you observe them. Many animals will not return to their home if they can tell (by the scent) that human beings have been there. And, of course, you should never kill or damage a plant or animal in your nature studies.

There are other places to study nature. Most cities have zoos where visitors can see unusual and exotic animals. You can also visit an aquarium, a kind of "zoo" for fish and other animals that live in water. If you are interested in botany (the study of plants), you may want to visit botanical gardens where many varieties of trees, shrubs, flowers, and other

plants are grown. Planetariums have telescopes through which visitors can view the moon, stars, and planets. Many planetariums also show films on astronomy (the study of the heavens).

Outdoor Projects You will need some simple equipment for outdoor nature study. A small magnifying glass, or hand lens, is very useful for examining insects, veins in leaves, pollen or flowers, and mineral grains that make up some rocks. In order to learn from your observations, you will also need a notebook. You should record in it plant and animal descriptions, unusual animal habits, the locations of things observed, and the time you observed them. You may also want to take an inexpensive *magnetic compass*. It will give you directions that you can write in your note-

▼ *A shrimping net is useful for studying life in shallow water at low tide. If you are lucky, you may catch numerous shrimps and some small fish.*

book to help describe the location of interesting things, and it may keep you from becoming lost. You will need a couple of glass jars and a sturdy *canvas bag* for collecting things and carrying them home. A small, lightweight *spade* may also be useful for outdoor nature study.

Nature Walk Perhaps you think you cannot learn much about nature from the area you live in. But even the smallest yard or park can teach you a great deal about plants and animals. Gather your equipment and go for a walk through a nearby park, field, meadow, or other wooded area. Try to identify the kinds of trees you see. Are they mostly evergreens or deciduous trees (trees that lose their leaves in autumn)? If you are walking in the spring or summer, notice whether any of the trees bear flowers or fruit. If you cannot tell a tree by its flower or fruit, put a sample in your bag to identify later. If you are walking in the autumn, notice whether the leaves on the trees have turned, and if so, to what color. Notice which trees have lost most of their leaves and which have kept most of theirs. Write in your notebook what some of the most interesting trees look like. Is the bark on the tree smooth or rough? What color is it? Do the branches grow out of the tree trunk just above the ground or do they start high on the trunk? If you can, make a drawing of the tree. Then add one of its leaves to the collection in your bag.

Do you see any shrubs or flowers in the area? Write in your notebook what some of them look like. Are the shrubs blooming? Do they have green leaves? If the flowers are arranged in beds, they have been planted there. Do not pick any of them but try to identify as many as you can. Flowers such as tulips and daffodils are probably familiar to you. If the flowers seem to be growing at random through the area, they are probably wildflowers. It is best not to pick

them. In some states it is illegal.

If you walk quietly and slowly, you may be able to observe some small animals. (If you are noisy, they will run and hide before you see them.) You may see a bee crawling into a flower, searching for nectar. Watch the bee closely and see where it goes next. Does the bee go to another flower? If it does, you may be seeing a bee carrying pollen from a male to a female flower. You may see a squirrel burying an acorn or a bird bringing worms to her young. Try to identify as many animals as you can. Look for their homes, if you can do this without frightening the animals. Birds' nests and molehills are usually very easy to see.

If you walk through an area that has a pond or stream, look at the plants and animals living in the water. You may see water insects, algae and other plants, and small fish. If you have an aquarium or plan to make one, you may want to take some specimens home in a jar of water. Take home a gallon jar of pond water containing algae for an indoor project.

BIRD-WATCHING. Many people find bird-watching a fascinating part of nature study. You can observe birds—their appearance, habits, and habitats (where they live)—in the fields and woods or on nature trails.

▲ *Birds rely on a regular food source in winter, and a well-stocked bird feeder will bring them to your garden. It is not, however, a good idea to feed birds during the breeding season. Natural foods, especially insects, are better for them, and household scraps may even harm young birds.*

Louis Agassiz, the famous naturalist, always told his classes, "Study nature, not books."

▲ *Binoculars with a ×10 magnification and an object lens of 50 mm are useful for bird-watching in the open countryside.*

▲ *A small portable hide for bird photography can be constructed using a light metal frame and dull-colored waterproof material.*

BIRDWATCHING

Birdwatching can be as simple or as complicated as you like. It can be just observing and keeping records of the birds that come to a home bird feeder. At the other end of the scale, it can mean hours of patient but often rewarding observation requiring special equipment such as binoculars, telescopes, tape recorders, and cameras. You may choose to study one type of bird, or all the birds that live in a certain habitat. Keep a notebook handy to jot down details on the birds you see. For example, how big is the bird? What color are its tail and wings? What kind of beak and feet does it have? Does it eat seeds or insects? Make a note of its song, and a rough drawing of the bird if you can. After only a few months you may be surprised by the number of different bird species you have "collected."

▲ *In the field, it is a good idea to make notes of everything you see and hear (top). If you spot an unfamiliar bird you can look it up later in a reference book, using your notes and drawings as a guide. A rough sketch (above) of a bird, with labels for color, markings, beak shape, and any other details, is often more helpful for identification purposes than a long written description. The more details you have, the easier it will be to identify the bird you have seen.*

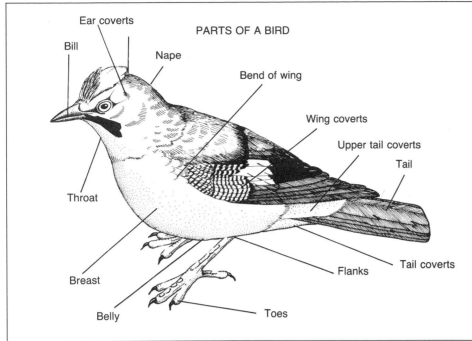

PARTS OF A BIRD

Ear coverts

Bill

Nape

Bend of wing

Wing coverts

Upper tail coverts

Tail

Throat

Breast

Belly

Toes

Flanks

Tail coverts

▼ *Compare these North American birds. The robin and the wood thrush are both in the thrush family. The lark bunting's beak is short and strong for breaking open seeds. The mockingbird can mimic calls of many other birds. The cactus wren has a sharp, pointed beak to catch insects.*

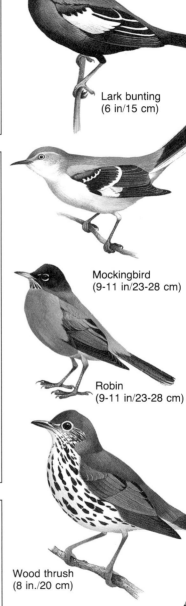

Lark bunting
(6 in/15 cm)

Mockingbird
(9-11 in/23-28 cm)

Robin
(9-11 in/23-28 cm)

Wood thrush
(8 in./20 cm)

Cactus wren
(7-9 in./18-23 cm)

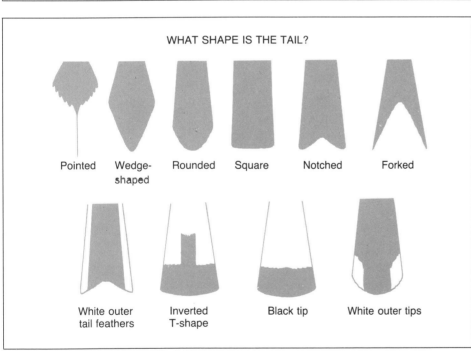

WHAT SHAPE IS THE TAIL?

Pointed Wedge-shaped Rounded Square Notched Forked

White outer tail feathers   Inverted T-shape   Black tip   White outer tips

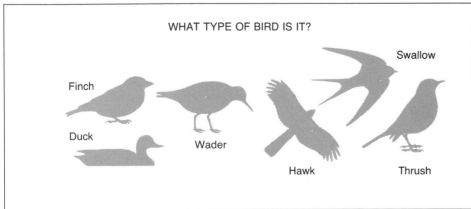

WHAT TYPE OF BIRD IS IT?

Finch

Duck

Wader

Swallow

Hawk

Thrush

NATURE STUDY

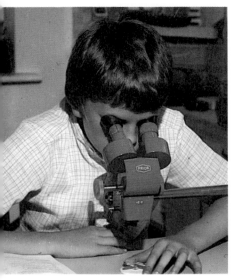

▲ *Binocular microscopes with a magnification of between 30 and 50 times are ideal for looking at, and identifying, small insects.*

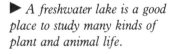

▶ *A freshwater lake is a good place to study many kinds of plant and animal life.*

(Binoculars will enable you to see the birds clearly from a distance so that you won't frighten them.) But it is fun to have birds near your home, where you can watch them whenever you want. You can attract birds to your home by putting food for them—birdseed, raisins, bits of bread—in your yard, spread on a bird feeder or on the ground. Make notes of the species of birds you observe. Be sure to include the date and where you saw the bird—was it in the fields, woods, in the garden, on or near water?

Many birds migrate to warmer parts of the world in winter. You may find that you live near a busy migratory route. In the fall, see if you can work out which birds are "just passing through." Make a note of them and see whether they return the following spring. Migrating geese often fly in a strict V-formation behind a leader. If you spot a flock of geese, listen to their calls and note which way they are heading.

Bird-watching during the breeding season can be tricky—be very careful not to disturb nesting birds. This is where a pair of binoculars is essential.

Indoor Projects PLANTS. Soon after your nature walk, go to a library and get books explaining the many kinds of trees, shrubs, and wildflowers. Handbooks have pictures of trees (or shrubs or flowers), their leaves, and any fruit a tree may bear. Beside each picture is information about the tree, shrub, or flower. You can look up the plant specimens you saw, using the notes or drawings you made, and find the names of the plants.

■ LEARN BY DOING

After you have studied plants growing outside, you may want to see more exactly *how* they grow. You can do this by growing plants from seeds. Growing herbs in window boxes is an easy project. Seeds of such herbs as basil, parsley, and sage are available in seed stores and many grocery stores. Follow the directions on the package and you will soon have a healthy crop of plants that are very useful—your parents can use them in cooking!

You can perform an interesting experiment with growing plants. Fill two flowerpots with soil and plant bean seeds in each. Put one pot in the sunlight—on a window ledge, for example. Put the other pot on the floor in the back of a dark closet. Water each pot often enough to keep the soil

damp to the touch. In about two weeks, you will notice that the plant growing in sunlight is green. The one growing in darkness is tall but has an unhealthy yellowish color. It grew very tall, probably in an effort to reach sunlight, but did not develop properly. This experiment shows the necessity of sunlight to plants. ■

ANIMALS. Human babies are clearly recognizable as human beings. But some living things, such as amphibians, have completely different forms at different times of their lives. Amphibians live the first part of their lives entirely in water. Then their form changes, and they spend the rest of their lives on both land and water. You can examine this change in one kind of amphibian, the frog.

■ LEARN BY DOING

In the spring, look in a pond for jellylike clumps attached to plants just below the surface of the water. Those clumps are frogs' eggs. Put the eggs into a bucket of pond water. Divide the eggs into four groups. Put each group into a separate dish. Put one dish on a high shelf near the ceiling. Put another dish on a table and the third on the floor. Put the fourth dish in a refrigerator. (The different locations will ensure different temperatures.) Keep all the dishes filled with pond water. Record in your notebook which dishes of eggs hatch and how many days it takes for most of the eggs to hatch.

While you are waiting for the eggs to hatch, prepare an aquarium. A large glass jar can be used for an aquarium. See the article on AQUARIUM for detailed directions.

The frogs' eggs will hatch into *tadpoles*, which look something like small fish. Put the tadpoles into the aquarium and watch them carefully. Look for changes in their form. Notice the feathery gills that will grow just behind their heads on both sides. The gills stick out, so they are easy to

see. Look for the hind legs and forelegs that soon develop. Notice how the color of the tadpoles changes. When most of the tadpoles have grown four legs, take them to the pond in which you found them and set them free. ■

If the tadpoles did not show much change by the end of two weeks, you probably took the eggs of a green frog or a bullfrog. The tadpoles of these two kinds of frogs will not complete their changes until the beginning of the second summer after they have hatched. These tadpoles should be returned to the pond where you found them.

If the tadpoles grow wartlike bumps on their skin, you have hatched the eggs of a toad. Although toads live on land, they lay their eggs in water—as all amphibians do.

For further information on:
Amphibians and Reptiles, *see* AMPHIBIAN, FROGS AND TOADS, LIZARD, METAMORPHOSIS, REPTILE, SALAMANDER, SNAKE, TURTLE.
Astronomy, *see* ASTEROID, ASTRONOMY, COMET, CONSTELLATION, DAY AND NIGHT, ECLIPSE, METEOR, MILKY

▲ *Find a tree that has recently been cut down and count the number of rings on the cut surface. Each ring of wood was formed during one year of the tree's growth, so by counting the rings you can tell how old the tree was when it was felled.*

▲ *A rock pool can be a fascinating place to observe shore life. This one contains mussels, a sea anemone, and a sea urchin which has camouflaged itself with small stones.*

TIONAL FOREST, NUT, PALM, PARASITIC PLANT, PHOTOSYNTHESIS, PLANT BREEDING, POISONOUS PLANT, ROSE, SEEDS AND FRUIT, SHRUB, TREE, WATER PLANT, WEED, WILDFLOWER.

Rocks and Minerals, *see* DIAMOND, GEM, GLASS, GOLD, GRANITE, MINERAL, ROCK, SILVER, SOIL, URANIUM.

Weather, *see* AIR, AIR PRESSURE, ATMOSPHERE, BAROMETER, CLIMATE, CLOUD, FOG, FROST, HAIL, HUMIDITY, HURRICANE, LIGHTNING AND THUNDER, RAIN AND SNOW, SKY, TORNADO, WATER CYCLE, WEATHER, WIND.

WAY, MOON, NORTH STAR, OBSERVATORY, PLANETARIUM, SOLAR SYSTEM, STAR, SUN, TELESCOPE, UNIVERSE.

Biology, *see* EGG, INCUBATOR, PROTECTIVE COLORING, REPRODUCTION.

Birds, *see* BIRD, BIRDS OF PREY, CRANE, DUCKS AND GEESE, FLIGHTLESS BIRDS, GAME BIRDS, GARDEN BIRD, GULLS AND TERNS, HUMMINGBIRD, OWL, PIGEON, SEABIRDS, SONGBIRDS, WATER BIRDS.

Environment, *see* ANIMAL DISTRIBUTION, ANIMAL HOMES, CITY WILDLIFE, ECOLOGY, FOOD WEB, MARINE LIFE, NATIONAL PARK, NATURAL RESOURCES, PLANT DISTRIBUTION, POND LIFE, SWAMPS AND MARSHES.

Insects, *see* ANT, BEE, BEETLE, BUG, BUTTERFLIES AND MOTHS, DRAGONFLY, DROSOPHILA, FLY, GRASSHOPPER, INSECT, SPIDER, WASPS AND HORNETS.

Mammals, *see article at name.*

Naturalists, *see* BURBANK, LUTHER; DARWIN, CHARLES; FABRE, JEAN; LINNAEUS, CAROLUS; MENDEL, GREGOR; WALLACE, ALFRED RUSSEL.

Nature Study Equipment, *see* AQUARIUM, MICROSCOPE, TERRARIUM.

Plants, *see* ALGAE, BARK, BOTANICAL GARDEN, BOTANY, BULB, CACTUS, CITRUS FRUIT, CLUB MOSS, CONIFER, EVERGREEN TREE, FERN, FLOWER, FUNGUS, GARDEN FLOWER, GARDENING, HORSETAIL, HOUSE PLANT, INSECT-EATING PLANT, LEAF, LICHEN, MOSSES AND LIVERWORTS, MUSHROOM, NA-

NAURU see MICRONESIA.

NAVAHO INDIANS The Navaho, or Navajo, Indians are the largest tribe in the United States today, with a population of more than 166,500 people. Most of them live on a large reservation located in parts of Arizona, New Mexico, and Utah.

The Navaho were wandering people who emigrated from the Canadian North to the southwest more than 500 years ago. At first the Navaho were raiders and warriors, but they learned farming from the Pueblo Indians. The Navaho also became herders,

▼ *This rare photograph of a Navaho male was taken in the 1880's. At this time the tribe was still low in numbers following the long warfare with the U.S. government.*

◀ *"The Indian Weaver" was painted by Robert Wesley Amick. Navaho Indians were weaving their highly regarded blankets, rugs, ponchos and dresses as early as the 1700's. They are noted for their beautiful colors and geometric designs.*

keeping flocks of sheep and goats and some cattle and horses.

During the 1700's and early 1800's, the Navaho often fought against the Spanish colonists and Mexicans. After the Mexican War, U.S. settlers moved into New Mexico demanding the Navaho's land. Other settlers on their way to California often stole from the Navaho's cornfields and flocks, killing many Indians while doing so.

The Navaho signed a peace treaty with the U.S. government in 1846. The Indians even returned some horses and sheep they had stolen. But while at the "peace conference," a U.S. soldier demanded one more horse! The Navaho started to ride off and were fired upon.

The Navaho and the U.S. government engaged in almost continuous warfare for the next 18 years. Despite their warlike reputation, the Navaho never practiced scalping. They would not go near a dead body because they feared evil spirits.

In 1863, Colonel Kit Carson and 700 soldiers were sent to the Southwest to "control" the nearly 10,000 Navaho. With the help of the Pueblo, the soldiers destroyed Navaho crops and cattle, causing widespread starvation. The tribe was reduced to about 7,000 people, and the survivors were captured and taken as prisoners to Fort Sumner on the Pecos River. There the tribe suffered severe hardships from disease, crop failures, and attacks from other tribes. They pleaded to be returned to their lands in New Mexico. A new treaty, signed in 1868, allowed the captives to return to an area on the border of Arizona and New Mexico that was set aside as a Navaho reservation. The tribe was given herds of sheep and goats. In 1884, the reservation was extended to provide more grazing room.

Each Navaho family lives by itself, rather than in villages. The traditional Navaho home is a one-room *hogan*, a cone-shaped house of logs covered with earth. It has a smoke hole at the top and is entered through a short, covered passage. The Navaho are skilled silversmiths and make beautiful jewelry from silver and turquoise. The fine, sturdy Navaho blankets are known throughout the world.

The Navaho's religion is based on their love of nature—the land, winds, and water. They believe that the gods of these natural things can influence human affairs. Ceremonial dances are performed in which the gods are represented by painted and masked men. Songs, chants, prayers, and colorful sand paintings are all part of their religious ceremonies.

Like most other Indian tribes in

Navaho National Monument contains three of the largest and most elaborately decorated cliff dwellings in the world. The 360 acre (146 hectare) monument is surrounded by the Navaho Indian Reservation in northern Arizona.

▲ *The traverse board helped sailors to work out how far they had sailed. The helmsman inserted pegs to show how many half-hour periods the ship had sailed on any particular course. Estimated speed was shown in the four rows of holes at the foot of the board.*

▶ *The astrolabe was a highly developed sighting instrument used by the Arabs. It could be used to fix positions on the Earth's surface, to tell the time, and to time sunrise and sunset.*

the United States today, the Navaho continue to have many problems with poverty, poor educational facilities, and lack of training to live in the modern-day world. The great differences in the Indian way of life and the life in the world outside the reservation make it hard for many of the young people to leave the reservation. Today, a sawmill on the Navaho reservation is used to turn trees into lumber. Companies that develop the oil, natural gas, and coal beneath the tribe's land pay the tribe for its use. From the Navaho capital at Window Rock, Arizona, tribal leaders plan how to better the lives of the Navaho Indians.

ALSO READ: CARSON, KIT; INDIAN ART, AMERICAN; INDIANS, AMERICAN; INDIAN WARS; MEXICAN WAR.

NAVIGATION How do you find your way to school or to a friend's house? How do you reach a playground the first time you go there? You get to school because you know the way, and you remember to turn left by a certain house. You find your way to a new place by following directions that tell you—in steps—what you must do to get where you want to go.

You can see that the people who guide airplanes and ships have the

same problem, only it is more complicated. How can you tell where you are or what to do next if your airplane is above the clouds or your ship is far from any land? Finding out is the work of navigation.

One of the most important tools a navigator has is a set of *charts*, carefully prepared maps that help the navigator find his or her position. But navigation is sometimes so simple that no maps are needed.

Sailors call the simplest navigation *piloting* or *pilotage*. In piloting, the navigator uses a map and steers the ship or airplane from one landmark to the next. A landmark may be a tall building, a lighthouse, a river, or anything else that stands out on the landscape. You do piloting when you follow directions. It is useful to a navigator, but only in clear weather when the ship is near land.

Another simple kind of navigation is *dead reckoning*. A navigator does this when he or she wants a good guess of the ship's or airplane's position. For example, a ship leaves New York Bay at 2 P.M. The ship's course is east, and its speed is 20 miles (32 km) an hour. At 5 P.M. the navigator checks the direction of the ship's course, how long the ship has been sailing, and its speed. Then he or she reckons that the ship is 60 miles (97 km) east of New York. This may not be exact, but it is accurate enough for many uses.

Two kinds of navigation are more complicated—celestial and electronic. *Celestial navigation* makes use of the fact that the sun and stars are always in certain positions depending on the time of day (or night) and the date of the year. Columbus and all the other famous explorers of the New World used the sun to guide them back to Europe.

To navigate by the sun or stars, a navigator uses a *sextant*. This device measures the angle between the sun (or a star) and the horizon. When the navigator knows this angle, he or she looks up the sun or star in a book of tables called the *American Ephemeris and Nautical Almanac*. From the sun angle, and the date and time, the navigator calculates the *approximate* position. By measuring the sun at two times several hours apart, he or she can get an *exact* position.

Electronic Navigation Navigators today use several radio and radar systems to help find their position. A simple system that airplanes use consists of radio signals broadcast from special towers at airports. When pilots are on an airway, they hear a steady hum. If they go off course, they hear "beeps."

Another system has the name LO-RAN, which comes from the words *long range na*vigation. Ocean-crossing airplanes use LORAN. Two radar units a few miles apart on land send a signal out to sea. The signals show up as two dots of light on the airplane's radar screen. The navigator turns a dial until the two dots become one, showing the airplane's position.

An even newer system for ships and planes makes use of Earth-orbiting satellites. Each satellite has a radio transmitter. The navigator tunes in the "beep" from a satellite, then uses a special computer to measure the angle between the satellite

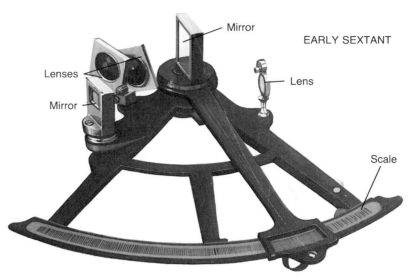

EARLY SEXTANT

Mirror

Lenses

Lens

Mirror

Scale

and the ship or plane. The computer then figures out the position of the ship or plane.

Other travelers, the astronauts, also have a problem knowing where they are. When a ship sails the ocean, the place the ship started from and the place it is going to do not move around with relation to each other. But when astronauts blast off for the moon, the Earth *and* the moon are both moving. How do the astronauts find their way to the moon and back again? They have a special sextant-telescope aboard the spacecraft. This instrument measures the angle between the Earth and a star and gives this information to a computer. The computer works out the spacecraft's position.

▲ *The sextant measures how high the sun or a star, such as the Pole Star, is above the horizon. From this measurement, and the time of the observation, the navigator can work out his position.*

People are not the only navigators. Animals have always traveled great distances to find food and to breed. Seals, turtles, and seabirds can navigate over thousands of miles of open ocean with amazing accuracy. How they do this is still rather a mystery.

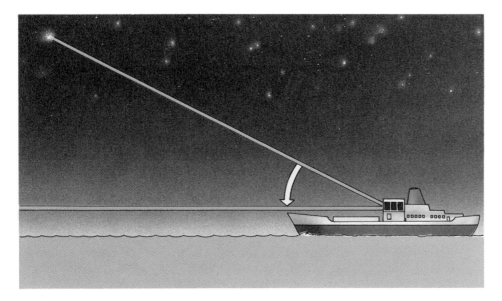

◄ *Various navigation aids help ships to determine their position. This ship is using a modern sextant, fixing its position by the height of a star above the horizon. Modern vessels can also check position in relation to certain artificial satellites, from radio signals beamed out by shore transmitters, or by radar echoes bounced off navigation buoys.*

▲ *This ship's wheelhouse has a wide range of navigational equipment.*

NAVY A navy is a nation's military force that fights on water. In time of war, a navy protects its home shores and at the same time may attack an enemy's coastline and ships. A country's navy includes not only the ships and personnel, but also the naval docks and shipyards where boats are housed, repaired, and built. A navy also has supply depots, radar and intelligence equipment, and staffs of nonsailing people who coordinate the activities.

The ancient civilizations of Assyria, Egypt, Phoenicia, Greece, Carthage, and Rome built and maintained naval fleets. The first known sea battle took place in 664 B.C. between the Greeks and the people of Corcyra (the Mediterranean island now called Corfu). The Greeks built large ships called *triremes*. A trireme had three rows of oars on each side of the ship. A heavy, pointed piece of

How to Get There from Here? Knowing his or her position is only the first half of a navigator's job. The second half is getting the ship where it is supposed to go.

The navigator uses charts to do this. On each of these maps is a network of imaginary lines. Lines of *longitude* run north-south. Lines of *latitude* run east-west. Each point on the Earth has its own position in terms of latitude and longitude. For example, if you look at a map of the United States, you will see that the latitude line marked 41 degrees north and the longitude line marked 74 degrees west meet at New York City. No other spot on Earth has this position.

When navigators know their position, they draw a line from the spot to the spot they want to go to. This line is the *course*. Most courses are not really straight lines. Ships must avoid storms and sail around islands. Airplanes, too, fly away from bad weather. Navigators then learn their new position and set a new course.

ALSO READ: COMPASS, LATITUDE AND LONGITUDE, MAP, RADAR, RADIO.

wood jutted out underwater from the front, or *prow*, of the ship to ram enemy ships.

From the A.D. 900's to the 1100's, the Vikings (the Norse people) formed a powerful sea force. They used light, fast-moving ships that could be either rowed or sailed. Small groups of Norse ships attacked the coastal and river cities of Europe. Their skill at navigation enabled them to reach the coast of Newfoundland around the year 1000. During the Middle Ages, European countries built up their own navies to protect themselves against the Vikings. Spain had one of the strongest European navies during the 1400's and 1500's. The main boat used for fighting was the *galleon*—a tall, wooden ship built to hold the weight of heavy guns. The gun barrels pointed out from portholes in the sides of the galleon. Ships had to draw up parallel to each other in order to fire on one another. In 1588, the Spanish Armada (a fleet of warships) was sent against England. The Spanish fleet was defeated.

In the 1500's shipbuilders began to experiment with ways to protect warships. All ships were made of wood, and when they were hit by gunfire, they burned easily. In 1530, a Spanish ship called the *Santa Anna* was entirely covered with lead and put to sea. Lead made the vessel heavy and hard to move, since its only power came from the force of wind or the pulling of oars. In 1782, the French built ten ships that were protected on one side with *turtleback*—a covering of wooden beams and layers of leather and cork, held together with iron bars.

In 1814, Robert Fulton built the first steam-powered warship, the *Desmologos*. The French ship, *Gloire*, launched in 1859, was the first *ironclad*. The ironclads were steam-powered, wooden ships, covered with

▼ *Life below decks in the navies of several centuries ago was very different from naval life today. Here, on the gun deck of a galleon, men rush to reload the cannons in a close atmosphere of smoke and little light or air.*

▲ *The first ironclad frigate was the French* La Gloire. *Its wooden hull was armored with 4-inch (11.4-cm) plate.*

▲ *The British ship HMS* Dreadnought *was the latest in battleship design when it appeared in 1906. It carried ten 12-inch (30-cm) guns, and was armored with 11 inches (28 cm) of toughened steel plate.*

▲ *The American aircraft carrier U.S.S.* Enterprise *and her escorts. At 1,100 feet (335 m), the* Enterprise *is the world's longest warship.*

sheets of iron. They were *fully rigged* (had a full set of sails) so that they could use the power of the wind as well as the power of their engines. During the U.S. Civil War, both the Confederate and Union navies had ironclad ships, called the *Monitor* and the *Merrimack*.

As engines became more powerful and guns became heavier and more deadly, ships were built entirely of metal. By the end of World War I, every large navy was using steel battleships and cruisers. The German navy made heavy use of submarines during World War I. The U.S. Navy developed aircraft carriers, a powerful force during World War II.

Navies have various kinds of ships that do different jobs. *Aircraft carriers* are the biggest. They carry heavy guns and act as floating airstrips and launch pads for planes and helicopters. The planes carry bombs, missiles, and guns for use against the enemy. *Battleships* are next largest in size, although they are rarely used nowadays, being largely replaced by aircraft carriers. They are protected with thick armor and carry big, heavy guns to hit long-range targets. *Cruisers*, also rarely used now, are lighter than battleships and do not have so many big guns. *Destroyers* are small, fast ships carrying all kinds of guns. They are not so heavily armored as battleships and can move quickly to attack and escape. *Submarines* move under water. The new ones carry missiles and are powered by nuclear energy. *Minelayers* plant *mines* (underwater explosives) for use against enemy shipping. *Minesweepers* locate and destroy mines that the enemy has planted. *Frigates* are small ships used mostly for *escort* (guiding and protecting other ships). *Transport ships* carry personnel and supplies. Many other ships, such as PT (torpedo) boats and icebreakers do special jobs for a navy.

The United States Navy During the American Revolution, General

George Washington *commissioned* (put into service) seven ships to seize British vessels carrying troops and supplies. These seven ships, along with merchant vessels and the naval ships of each colony, were combined in 1775 to form the Continental Navy. In 1785, the Continental Navy was discontinued and the ships sold to merchants and private mariners. In 1798, Congress established the Department of the Navy. The Navy was ordered to protect U.S. ships from piracy.

In the War of 1812, the Navy was strengthened and U.S. ships won some important naval battles against the British. After the War of 1812, the U.S. ships were also sent on voyages of exploration to Antarctica and the South Pacific Ocean. The Navy played an important part in the Mexican War, supplying troops and equipment to the U.S. Army fighting in Mexico. In 1850, Commodore Matthew Perry headed a naval expedition to Japan that resulted in trade agreements with that country.

During the Civil War, the U.S. Navy *blockaded* (prevented ships from entering or leaving) Southern ports. This kept the Confederate States from selling their goods abroad, and it also kept foreign countries from sending troops and supplies to the Confederate forces. In 1883, the first all-steel ships were built for the U.S. Navy. The steel battleship, *Maine*, was blown up and sunk in the harbor of Havana, Cuba, in 1898. This disaster started the Spanish-American War in which the Navy's powerful steel battleships defeated the Spanish fleet. From 1900 to 1910, the Navy conducted scientific expeditions that led to reaching the North Pole in 1909.

The Navy's main job in World War I was to ship troops and supplies to Europe and to fight German submarines. Great mine fields were laid. Naval pilots flew a total of almost a million miles (1.6 million km), watch-

ing for German submarine activity. The Japanese bombing of the U.S. naval base at Pearl Harbor brought the United States into World War II. The Navy was most active in the Pacific Ocean. Naval troops called "Seabees" rapidly built bases and airstrips on conquered islands. U.S. submarines kept supplies from reaching Japan by destroying Japanese trading vessels. U.S. aircraft carriers moved swiftly defeating the Japanese with their combined strength of sea and air power.

Battleships were an important force in World War II. Since then, aircraft carriers, with their ability to strike at longer distances by using airplanes instead of guns, have replaced battleships. U.S. aircraft carriers were used in the Korean and Vietnam wars.

The U.S. Navy has three sections. The *Operating Forces* include the fleets and all forces operating on the sea, as well as the U.S. Coast Guard in time of war. The *Navy Department* includes all people working on naval business and research. The *Shore Establishment* includes all Naval and Marine Corps men and women not working at sea or in the Navy Department.

▲ *The United States Navy patrols many parts of the world, ensuring the safe and free passage of passenger and cargo ships in international waters. A strong naval presence in a sensitive area such as the Middle East or Persian Gulf, can also ensure stability during a crisis.*

The greatest naval invasion was the Allied landing on the French coast on D day, June 6, 1944. During the first three days of the landing, 745 ships and over 4,000 landing craft took part.

▲ *The battleship U.S.S. New Jersey firing her 16-inch (406-mm) guns exemplifies the old type of gun-armed ship. Their only use now is for shore bombardment.*

▶ *Modern aircraft carriers are floating bases from which land and air assaults can be launched.*

▼ *The Lockheed S-3 Viking is a carrier-based aircraft operated by the U.S. Navy. The aircraft's high-set, slightly swept wings, large fin, and the closeness of the engines to the fuselage, make it easy to recognize.*

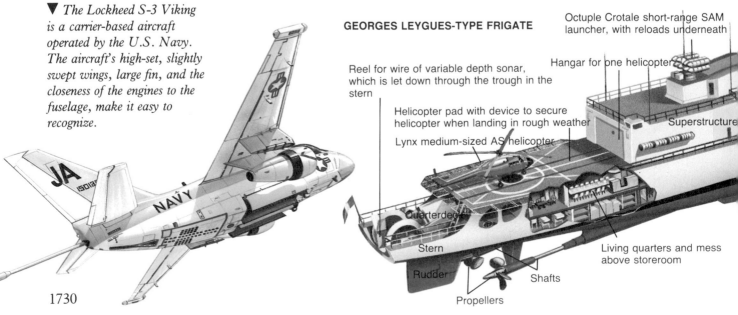

GEORGES LEYGUES-TYPE FRIGATE

Octuple Crotale short-range SAM launcher, with reloads underneath

Hangar for one helicopter

Reel for wire of variable depth sonar, which is let down through the trough in the stern

Helicopter pad with device to secure helicopter when landing in rough weather

Superstructure

Lynx medium-sized AS helicopter

Quarterdeck

Stern

Living quarters and mess above storeroom

Rudder

Shafts

Propellers

In 1942, the WAVES (Women Appointed for Voluntary Emergency Service) was organized as a women's branch of the Navy during World War II. They then became part of the regular Navy.

The Department of the Navy is part of the Department of Defense and is headed by the Secretary of the Navy, a civilian appointed by the President. The President's naval adviser is the Chief of Naval Operations, who directs leaders of the Marine Corps and the Coast Guard. Young men and women who join the Navy can arrange to study for a college degree or receive special training in skills that can help them build good careers. Even aboard one large aircraft carrier there is a wide variety of careers available.

ALSO READ: AIRCRAFT CARRIER; AMERICAN REVOLUTION; BYRD, RICHARD E.; CIVIL WAR; COAST GUARD; GUNS AND RIFLES; JONES, JOHN PAUL; KOREAN WAR; MARINE CORPS; MISSILE; MONITOR AND MERRIMACK; NAVIGATION; PEARL HARBOR; PERRY, OLIVER HAZARD; PIRATES AND PRIVATEERS; SHIPS AND SHIPPING; SPANISH ARMADA; SUBMARINES; U.S. SERVICE ACADEMIES; VIETNAM WAR; WAR OF 1812; WORLD WAR I; WORLD WAR II.

NEBRASKA The long Platte River flows through the state of Nebraska. The people traveling west in covered wagons used to say jokingly, "that river is a mile [1.6 km] wide and an inch [2.5 cm] deep." The Platte River is very shallow during the dry summer season. And it has a wide, flat bed. So the Omaha and Oto Indians called it *Nebrathka*, "flat water." The name of the state comes from this Indian name for the river.

The Land and Climate Nebraska lies in the central part of the continental United States. South Dakota is its northern neighbor. Kansas is on the south. Iowa lies on the east, across the

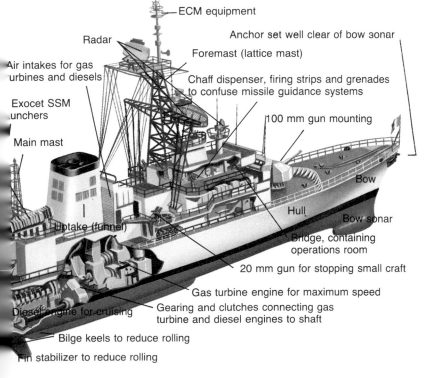

▲ *A modern frigate is equipped for speed, with the latest in radar, sonar, missile launchers, and electronic systems.*

	Fleet Admiral
	Admiral
	Vice Admiral
	Rear Admiral
	Commodore
	Captain
	Commander
	Lieutenant Commander
	Lieutenant
	Lieutenant Junior Grade
	Ensign
	Chief Warrant Officer W-4
	Chief Warrant Officer W-3
	Chief Warrant Officer W-2
	Warrant Officer W-1
	Master Chief Petty Officer of the Navy
	Master Chief Petty Officer
	Senior Chief Petty Officer
	Chief Petty Officer
	Petty Officer First Class
	Petty Officer Second Class
	Petty Officer Third Class
	Seaman
	Seaman Apprentice
	Seaman Recruit

▲ *Toadstool Geological Park near Crawford, Nebraska, is a fascinating wonderland of strangely shaped rock formations. Some of them look like giant toadstools.*

Arbor Day, when trees are planted, was first celebrated in Nebraska in 1872. The idea was suggested by J. Sterling Morton of Arbor Lodge, Nebraska City.

Missouri River. Nebraska's western neighbors are Wyoming and Colorado.

Plains cover Nebraska. They belong mostly to the Great Plains, but a different kind of plains is found in the eastern fifth of the state. These eastern Till Plains are part of the rich prairie country that lies south and west of the Great Lakes. Both kinds of plains were almost treeless before white settlers came to the area.

The northwestern part of Nebraska is a region of low sand hills. The Sand Hills end in the west. Nebraska's high plains and mountains rise near Wyoming. The central and eastern parts of the state are dissected (cut up) by streams. Between them are hills with long, gentle slopes.

Precipitation is light in most of western Nebraska. The eastern part of the state receives more rain. All of Nebraska is hot in summer. In the high western part, though, summer nights are cool. Nebraska winters are cold. But in the western part, a winter wind, called a *chinook*, sometimes brings milder weather. This warm, dry wind blows along the eastern edge of the Rocky Mountains. Chinooks can melt snow even in midwinter.

History Indians and white settlers saw Nebraska very differently. For years, white people thought of it only as country to travel through on the way to somewhere else. But Indians thought it was a wonderful place to live. The difference in viewpoint was due to differences in occupation. Most of the white settlers were farmers. Nebraska did not have enough rain for their crops. The Indians were hunters. The grass of the Great Plains and the prairie fed vast herds of buffalo (bison). These animals provided the Indians with meat, warm robes, and material for clothing. Bison hides were used in making tipis (tents). Pronghorn antelope and jackrabbits were also plentiful, and the Indians hunted them for food. The Plains Indians were fighters, as well as hunters. The Pawnee, an especially warlike tribe, were almost always fighting against the other tribes of Nebraska. Among these were the Sioux, Cheyenne, Omaha, Oto, Ponca, and Arapaho.

Nebraska was part of the huge territory claimed by France in 1682. It interested only those French who bought furs from Indians. No settlements were started. France sold Nebraska to the United States in 1803, as part of the Louisiana Territory. Americans then came to explore parts of Nebraska, but they were simply mapping routes west.

The Oregon Trail, which passed through Nebraska, became one of the chief migration routes. Covered wagons creaked slowly alongside the Platte and North Platte rivers. The wagon trains stopped for one or two nights at a time. But no one—except American fur traders—stayed in the area. This wilderness of grass and sky did not attract settlers. The fur traders themselves stayed close to the Missouri River. River steamboats carried their furs away and brought them goods from the East. The river port of Omaha was founded in 1854. In this little town, pioneers bought supplies for their journey west.

Few settlers lived in the Nebraska region at the time of the Civil War. The United States government tried to encourage settlement by offering free or very inexpensive land there to

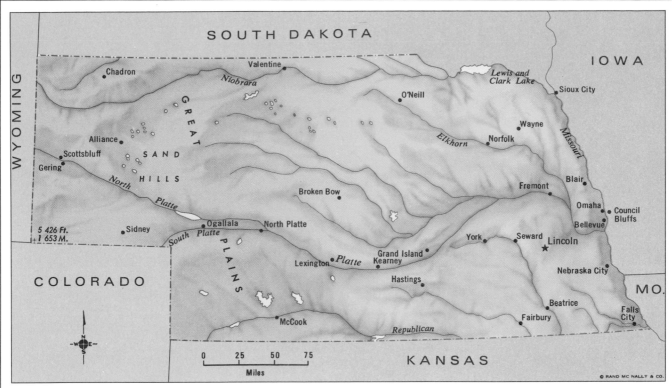

NEBRASKA

Capital
Lincoln (189,000 people).

Area
77,227 square miles (200,000 sq. km)
Rank: 15th

Population
1,607,000 people
Rank: 36th

Statehood
March 1, 1867
(37th state admitted)

Principal river
Platte River

Highest point
5,424 feet (1,653 m) in Kimball County

Largest city
Omaha
(355,000 people)

Motto
Equality before the Law

Song
"Beautiful Nebraska"

Famous people
Fred Astaire, Willa Cather, "Buffalo Bill" Cody, Henry Fonda, Gerald R. Ford, General John J. Pershing, Malcolm X.

STATE EMBLEMS

Cottonwood

Western Meadowlark

Goldenrod

NEBRASKA

▶ *The Sand Hills region of Nebraska is a perfect area for rearing cattle because of the fine grasses and abundant water supply.*

In 1883, Buffalo Bill (William Cody) organized his famous Wild West Show at his ranch near North Platte, Nebraska.

people who would farm it. There were few takers at first, but after the war there were more. Many former soldiers could not find work, and they wanted farms. The new Union Pacific Railroad made travel to Nebraska easy. Also, Nebraska had become a state. For these reasons, more people settled there. To protect settlers, the government made agreements with the Indians. Most tribes gave up their lands. But the Sioux and the Cheyenne fought until they were defeated in the late 1870's. The new settlers had a very hard time. Drought often ruined crops. In some years, grasshoppers ate everything. Winter blizzards killed cattle. And there was no timber on the treeless plains for building houses. Ranchers and farmers built cabins with blocks of sod cut from the plain. Farmers learned to use irrigation and dry farming methods in the 1890's, but farming troubles continued through the 1930's.

Willa Cather, one of the greatest American writers, grew up in Nebraska during the early farming days. Her novel, *My Ántonia*, is a touching story of a Czech family that immigrated to Nebraska and worked hard to farm the land.

Nebraskans at Work World War II brought Nebraska farmers new prosperity. The Missouri River Basin

Project, begun in 1949, provides for irrigation and flood control in Nebraska. Agriculture is now the state's leading business. Corn is the biggest crop. It is raised in eastern and central Nebraska. Farther west, where the rainfall is lighter, hay and wheat are grown. Livestock earns much more money than crops. Beef cattle are the state's most valuable animals. They graze widely in the Sand Hills region. Sheep, hogs, turkeys, and chickens are also raised.

Manufacturing is Nebraska's second biggest business. The principal products are foods. Omaha is one of the nation's largest food-processing centers. It has big meat-packing plants and canning factories. Tourism earns many millions of dollars every year. Tourists visit the Scotts Bluff National Monument above the North Platte River. This tall, rocky landmark once guided westward bound travelers along the Oregon Trail. At Minden near Hastings, Nebraska, there is a model pioneer village with a pony express station. Other tourist attractions include Buffalo Bill's Scouts Rest Ranch near North Platte and the Stuhr Museum of the Prairie Pioneer near Grand Island. Boys Town near Omaha is visited too. Bison and elk roam at Fort Niobrara National Wildlife Refuge.

Nebraska is the only state in the United States to have a *unicameral*

▼ *Memorial Stadium, Lincoln, Nebraska.*

(one-house) legislature. State law-makers belong to no party.

ALSO READ: GREAT PLAINS, LOUISIANA PURCHASE, PAWNEE INDIANS, PRAIRIE, WESTWARD MOVEMENT.

NEEDLEWORK

NEEDLEWORK Most people agree that needlework includes embroidery, needlepoint, cross-stitch, petit point, crewel, appliqué, quilting, and tapestry. Some say that hemstitching ("drawn threadwork"), knitting, crocheting, tatting, lace making, and fine hand sewing—even of garments—are other types of needlework. Needlework may also include rug hooking and weaving.

It is generally agreed that needlework refers to work done primarily for beauty rather than usefulness. Some people call it "art needlework," to separate it from plain sewing. However, many needlework products are also useful.

Ancient Needlework Needlework is an ancient craft. Egyptian cloth preserved from the 1400's B.C. shows both designs woven into the material and decorations stitched onto the fabric. Clothing taken from Crimean graves of the 300's B.C. are kept in a museum in Leningrad. They show silk, wood, and metallic threads on linen. A Viennese museum has a cloak, dated 1134, all sewn with silk, pearls, and precious stones.

Tapestry, or hand weaving, was used to decorate the walls of stone castles. Needleworkers became skillful in working beautiful designs into huge hangings of tapestry. The Bayeux Tapestry, made shortly after the Battle of Hastings in 1066, measures 230 feet (70 m) long and 20 inches (50 cm) wide. The tapestry shows many scenes leading up to and including the battle in which the Normans, led by William the Conqueror, defeated the Saxons under Harold.

Women in medieval courts spent years embroidering royal gowns and church vestments. Needlework styles emerged in each country. English women, especially during the reign of Elizabeth I (1533–1603), made heavy, ornate designs in strong colors. French workers preferred light, graceful stitches, often in white thread on white fabric. The Italians exported books of needlework patterns and spread the use of bright colors to other countries. Oriental work displayed gold and silver threads on silk, picturing dragons and fancy birds and flowers.

American Needlework The needlework crafts European settlers brought to America were not the first on the continent. Indians had already developed needlework using colored fibers, porcupine quills, and beads. Samplers (the framed wall hangings consisting of a piece of lightweight fabric with an embroidered picture and message) were done in colonial days, not for decoration, but to teach little girls to stitch. Embroidering the alphabet, numbers, and mottoes were a

▲ *The rich colors and geometrical pattern of this piece of silk embroidery are typical of many Islamic designs. It is from the Caucasus region of the Middle East, and dates from the 1700's.*

▼ *This beaded prayer-book cover is a fine example of Polish needlework of the 1500's. The bird is the national symbol of Poland.*

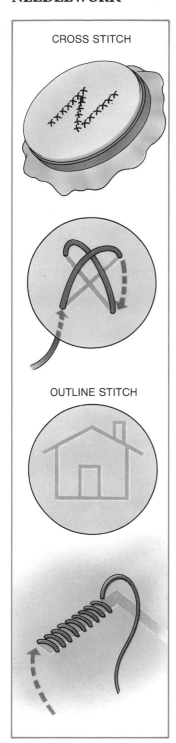

CROSS STITCH

OUTLINE STITCH

colonial girl's introduction to the skills of a homemaker.

The straight lines and tiny stitches used in samplers are only one kind of American stitchery. Waves of immigrants over the years brought new designs and various types of stitches. Today, the American needleworker has a world of styles to choose from.

Needlework, in any of its types, makes an enjoyable and instructive hobby. A needlework project can be done a little at a time, after school or before bedtime. The stitches should be simple at first. Even a beginner can add personal touches to a wardrobe, or a room, by stitching initials or other designs onto scarves, blouses, shirts, pillowcases, and towels.

■ LEARN BY DOING

Beginners in embroidery often make samples from fabric purchased with the design or pattern printed on it. This is a good way to practice the embroidery stitches before making your own pattern. The small x's on the pattern indicate that you should use the *cross-stitch* there. Bring the needle up through the fabric at an x'd pattern marking, leaving the knot on the wrong side of the fabric. The cross-stitch is made simply by sewing an x in the marked place. Cross-stitching is used for the letters and parts of the picture. Outlines on the design, such as houses or flower stems, are made with the *outline stitch*. Thread your needle as before and make a series of small, slanted stitches backward, leaving no gaps of fabric between the stitches.

▲ *An American cross-stitch sampler from the early 1800's. It was created by a young girl to show her skill at needlework.*

When you have mastered these two stitches, you may want to try making your own pattern. Put a piece of carbon paper face down on the fabric you plan to use. Draw your design with a pencil or pen on the carbon paper. When you lift the paper, you will see your design printed on the fabric. Then follow your own design as you would any other pattern.

Here is a simple piece you may want to try:

You can make an embroidered initial using the *satin stitch* by drawing a letter like the ones shown here. Transfer it to the fabric by drawing over carbon paper.

Start at one side of the design. Bring the needle up through the fabric, leaving the knot on the wrong side. Insert the needle down through the fabric directly across the design on the carbon mark. Now carry the needle across underneath the fabric and bring it up again very close to the first stitch. Repeat until the letter is completely filled. End by turning the fabric over and making three or four tiny running stitches through the fabric (not through threads). Clip the thread. Press with a warm iron on the wrong side of the fabric. ■

ALSO READ: LACE, SEWING.

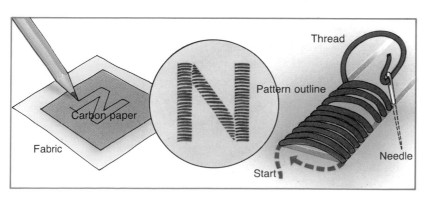

Thread

Pattern outline

Carbon paper

Fabric

Needle

Start

NEGRO HISTORY see BLACK AMERICANS.

NEHRU, JAWAHARLAL (1889–1964) In 1947, as the time grew near for India's independence from Great Britain, fighting was raging throughout the country between the followers of the Hindu and Muslim religions. Some people felt the new nation would not be able to survive. Excited crowds gathered in Delhi, the capital of India. Jawaharlal Nehru, calm and handsome, wearing a red rose in his buttonhole, came out to talk to the people. "As long as there are tears and suffering," he said, "so long our work will not be over. . .we have to build the noble mansion of free India where all her children may dwell . . . ."

Jawaharlal Nehru, India's first prime minister, was born in Allahabad. He was the only son of a wealthy high-caste (upper class) family. Young Jawaharlal was sent to school in England and graduated from Cambridge University. When he returned, he entered Indian politics. The entire family, including Jawaharlal's father, Motilal, worked closely with the Indian political leader, Mahatma Gandhi, in the struggle for Indian independence. In 1929, Nehru became president of the Indian National Congress, which led the struggle for independence from Britain. He was jailed several times for his actions against the British. While in prison, he wrote a book entitled *Glimpses of World History*.

Nehru believed that democracy was the best form of government for India. His chief aim as prime minister was to unite the country and improve the lives of the Indian people. He encouraged modern industry and new farming methods in the country. Nehru spoke out against war and aggression in the world. He made India a neutral country, not support-ing any of the great world powers. But in 1962, India fought a short war with China over a quarrel about the border between the two countries. When Nehru died, he was recognized throughout the world as one of the outstanding leaders of the century.

His daughter, Indira Gandhi, was India's prime minister for many years, but was assassinated in 1984. She was succeeded by her son, Nehru's grandson, Rajiv Gandhi. He too was assassinated, in 1991. His successor was P.V. Narasimha.

ALSO READ: GANDHI, INDIRA; GANDHI, MAHATMA; INDIA.

▲ *Jawaharlal Nehru, India's first prime minister.*

NELSON, HORATIO (1758–1805) The English admiral, Horatio Nelson, is considered Great Britain's most famous naval hero. Nelson joined the Royal Navy at the age of 12. He was captain of his own ship by the age of 20. In one battle, Nelson lost the sight of his right eye and in another, he lost his right arm. He won many famous victories against the French navy during the long war that the British fought against the French emperor, Napoleon I.

At the beginning of this war, the British were afraid that Napoleon might invade Britain with his army. Horatio Nelson was then admiral of the British fleet of ships in the Mediterranean Sea. His job was to stop the French fleet in the Mediterranean from joining their allies (friends), the Spanish fleet, which was in the Atlantic Ocean. If the French and Spanish ships joined together, they might successfully invade Britain.

The French fleet managed to slip out of the Mediterranean. But on October 21, 1805, Nelson trapped the French and Spanish fleets off the coast of Spain, near a place called Cape Trafalgar. In the famous Battle of Trafalgar, the British navy destroyed most of the French and Spanish ships. After this victory, Great

Just before the Battle of Trafalgar, Nelson hoisted his famous flag signal to the fleet: "England expects that every man will do his duty." As he lay dying after the battle, his last words were: "Thank God I have done my duty."

▲ *Admiral Nelson, who died at the Battle of Trafalgar in which Napoleon's fleet was defeated.*

A yak grazes near a temple in Nepal. In the background are the high peaks of the Himalaya Mountains.

Britain became the strongest naval power in Europe. But Nelson was killed during the battle.

Nelson is remembered most for his great bravery. One story tells how the British were being defeated in a sea battle and the commander of the fleet gave the signal to stop fighting. But Nelson put his telescope to his blind eye and said, "I really do not see the signal." His brave stand encouraged the fleet, and the British won the battle.

The British named Trafalgar Square, in London, in honor of the victory at Trafalgar. In the square is a column with a statue of Nelson on top.

ALSO READ: ENGLISH HISTORY.

NEPAL Nepal is a small kingdom that lies between India and Tibet in south central Asia. It is about the same size as the state of Wisconsin.

Many of the world's highest mountains, rising more than 26,000 feet (7,900 m) above sea level, are located in Nepal. Mount Everest, the world's highest peak, stands on Nepal's border with Tibet. Mount Kanchenjunga, the world's third highest mountain, is on Nepal's border with India. These peaks are part of the great Himalayan Mountains, which cover almost the whole of Nepal. The scenery of Nepal is spectacular, with snow-covered peaks, deep gorges, valleys of waving rice, and beautifully decorated palaces and Buddhist temples. The Karnali, Kosi, and Gandak rivers begin in the Himalayas of Nepal and flow south into India. The people, such as the Sherpas, who live in the mountains, are able to withstand the bitter cold and to breathe the thin air. But the climate in the lowland areas is mild. (See the map with the article on CHINA.)

Katmandu, the capital of Nepal, is located in a fertile valley in the center of the country. Most Nepalese cultivate small farms in valleys or lowland regions. They raise crops such as rice, wheat, corn, barley, and tobacco. They also keep herds of sheep and yaks, a type of ox. Nepalese houses are usually built of sun-dried bricks. Very few roads have been built in Nepal, and in some places elephants are still used for transportation.

Almost all the Nepalese follow either the Buddhist or the Hindu religions. Nepal is a sacred place for the Buddhists, as it is the birthplace of Buddha. The mighty mountains of Nepal separated the country from the rest of the world for centuries. In 1956, a new road connected India with Nepal and changes gradually came. Trade with other countries was developed, and tourists were encouraged for the first time to visit Nepal. The king of Nepal governs the country and is advised by a council of ministers and a national assembly elected by district, town, and village councils (panchayats).

ALSO READ: HIMALAYA MOUNTAINS.

NEPAL

Capital City: Katmandu (435,000 people).
Area: 54,362 square miles (140,787 sq. km).
Population: 17,000,000.
Government: Monarchy.
Natural Resources: Quartz, hydroelectric potential, small mineral resources.
Export Products: Clothing, carpets, leather goods, grain.
Unit of Money: Rupee.
Official Language: Nepali.

NERO (A.D. 37–68) Nero is remembered as one of the cruelest and most irresponsible of the Roman emperors. His mother married her uncle, Emperor Claudius, in A.D. 49. Claudius adopted Nero, and when he died Nero became emperor. At first, Nero left the business of government to his wise counselors. He was more interested in music, poetry, and acting. But after a few years, Nero seized power for himself. He had Claudius' son, his own mother, and even his wife, murdered. Nero's second wife, Poppaea, had a strong influence over the emperor. She probably encouraged his cruelty to gain power for herself.

In A.D. 64, a terrible fire broke out in Rome. Nero is said to have watched it with great glee. He blamed the followers of the Christian religion for the fire and punished them savagely. Under Nero many Christians were thrown to the lions in the arena.

The Romans were forced to pay huge taxes to support the emperor's many extravagant projects. Nero was finally declared a public enemy and condemned to death. He fled from Rome and killed himself.

ALSO READ: ROMAN EMPIRE.

NERVOUS SYSTEM A living thing must have some way of making its parts work together. It must also be aware of what is happening around it and to it, not only to protect itself, but also to carry on the life process. The nervous system (a network of nerve cells, or *neurons*, working together) performs this task.

All many-celled animals have some type of nervous system. In vertebrate animals, the nervous system consists of the brain, the spinal cord, and the large, complicated network (web) of nerves that branch off from the brain and spinal cord.

The Nerve Cell Each neuron consists of a central portion, called the *cell body*, containing the nucleus. Slender, threadlike bodies called *dendrites* branch out from the cell body. From one point in the cell body, there extends a long thread, the *axon*, which ends in a number of very thin and delicate branches. Some axons are very short, but others may be as much as 3 or 4 feet (90 to 120 cm) long. The longest axons are the largest cells in the body. The larger neurons are about 1/2,500 of an inch (0.001 cm) thick, and the smallest are about 1/250,000 of an inch (0.00001 cm) thick.

Messenger System of the Body
The entire nervous system is made up of a series of neurons, arranged so that the branching threads at the end of an axon mingle with the dendrites next in line. But the dendrite and axon branches do not touch each other. The gap between the two is called a *synapse*. Messages travel through the neurons in the form of small electric currents, called *nerve impulses*; they pass across synapses through chemicals released at the nerve endings.

A neuron is a cell with extraordinary abilities. It can not only *receive* messages from the sense organs, but it can also *transmit* (send) messages throughout the body. The dendrites receive messages and the axons transmit them. Nerve impulses moving along the nervous system are like messages traveling along telephone wires. Nerve impulses travel to and from the brain, which is like a telephone exchange, sorting out messages and sending them along the proper wires.

The simple act of picking up a pencil from the floor requires the work of millions of neurons. First, you must locate the pencil. Your nervous system "tells" your eye muscles to move your eyes and your neck muscles to turn your head. Once you have located the pencil, the muscles

▲ *Nero, the emperor who ruled so badly that he had to flee from Rome. He was more interested in music and the arts than in ruling justly, and the Romans rose up against his cruelty.*

There is a story that Nero set fire to Rome in A.D. 64 and fiddled while the city burned. Most historians doubt Nero's guilt. He certainly could not have played a violin as the instrument was not invented until the 1500's. If Nero played anything it was probably a lyre.

If you place your finger too near a lighted candle, the nerves in your finger relay the feeling of pain to your spinal column or brain. Pressure receptors (1) are buried deep in the skin. Touch receptors (2) are nearer the surface, as are cold (3) and heat (4) receptors. Pain receptors are simply free nerve endings (5). A nerve is a bundle of fibers, each of which is a neuron, or long cell. A motor neuron carries impulses from the brain to the muscles of your arm and shoulder, contracting them so that you pull your hand away from the flame.

in your arms, back, legs, and hands must act in the proper order (coordinate) to enable you to bend down, grasp the pencil, and straighten up again. You could not pick up the pencil if your fingers tried to grasp it before you bent down to reach it. The movements of your muscles and the order in which they act (coordination) are controlled by your nervous system.

Parts of the Nervous System The nervous system has two main divisions. The brain and spinal cord make up the *central nervous system*. Nerves that branch off from the spinal cord and go to all parts of the body make up the *peripheral nervous system*. (*Peripheral* means "away from the central part.") The brain is made up of billions of neurons with a vast number of connections between

them. All voluntary actions and mental activity start in the brain. The spinal cord is a long, thick bundle of nerves that runs from the brain to the lower part of the back. The spinal cord is the main pathway for messages traveling between the brain and the rest of the body. In a human being, 31 pairs of nerves branch off the spinal cord and then continue to branch out to all parts of the body.

SENSORY AND MOTOR NERVES. The relationship between the central and peripheral nervous systems may be seen in the way the body reacts to a sudden, painful irritation of the skin. If you touch a very hot object, you immediately jerk your hand away. You do not stop and think, "This is very hot. I will move my hand away." You act *automatically*. In this instance, special cells in the skin, called *receptors*, detected the heat. (Other receptors detect the pricking of a pin or the scratch of a nail, and so on.) The receptors carry the message to nearby neurons. The message travels along other neurons to the spinal cord. Nerves carrying messages from the sensory organs (eyes, ears, nose, etc.) are *sensory nerves*. When it reaches the spinal cord, the sensory impulse sets off an impulse in *motor nerves*, which carry messages to muscles, directing their movements. The impulse travels to your arm muscles, and you jerk your hand away from the object. This "automatic" movement is a *reflex*. The path traveled by the impulse—from skin to spinal cord to arm muscles—is called a *reflex arc*.

Reflexes are very valuable in protecting your body against harm. Suppose you had to stop to think about what to do every time you were threatened with harm. This would take time. Reflexes enable you to act quickly to protect yourself in harmful situations. Reflexes also help you to react to other situations besides pain or danger. Suppose someone throws a ball to you. Sensory nerves carry a picture of the approaching ball from

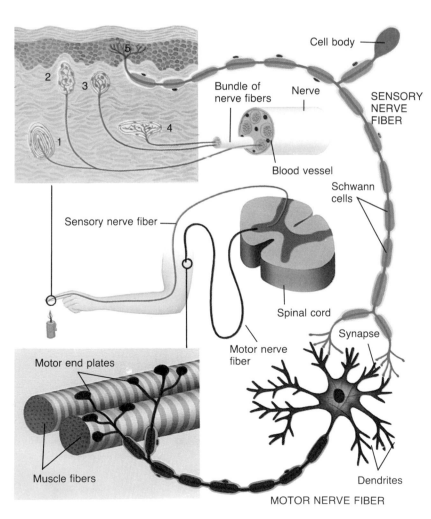

Cell body

Bundle of nerve fibers

Nerve

SENSORY NERVE FIBER

Blood vessel

Schwann cells

Sensory nerve fiber

Spinal cord

Synapse

Motor nerve fiber

Motor end plates

Muscle fibers

Dendrites

MOTOR NERVE FIBER

your eyes to your brain. The brain sends messages along motor nerves, directing muscles to raise your arms and open your hands.

AUTONOMIC NERVOUS SYSTEM. Many activities of the body that are necessary for life are carried on by the nervous system without any "thinking" at all. These activities are controlled by certain nerves of the peripheral nervous system, called the *autonomic nervous system*. These nerves control such functions as the movement of the lungs (respiration), the movement of the heart as it pumps blood (circulation), and the movement of the body organs as food is eaten and absorbed (digestion). The autonomic nervous system has two groups of nerves: *sympathetic* nerves (for "fight or flight") speed up certain body processes; *parasympathetic* nerves (for "rest or repair") slow down the same processes. Drugs, alcohol, and other substances such as caffeine in coffee, may stimulate these groups of nerves.

Diseases and Disorders of the Nervous System Unlike other cells in the body, nerve cells do not heal or replace themselves when they are damaged or destroyed. For this reason, diseases and injuries affecting the nervous system can easily result in the loss of the ability to control or perform body movements, loss of certain senses, and eventual paralysis. Diseases of the nervous system include infections, inflammations, and weakening of nerve cells. *Neurology* is the branch of medicine that deals with the structure and function of the nervous system. *Neurologists* treat diseases or disorders of the brain, spinal cord, and nerve cells.

ALSO READ: BIOCHEMISTRY, BRAIN, CELL, DISEASE, DRUG, HUMAN BODY, MENTAL HEALTH, MUSCLE, SENSE ORGAN.

NEST see BIRD.

NETHERLANDS The Netherlands is a small, flat country bordered by Belgium on the south and Germany on the east. (See the map with the article on EUROPE.) Part of the Netherlands is formed by the delta of the Rhine, Scheldt, Maas, Waal, and Lek rivers. Near the mouth of the Lek River lies Rotterdam, the busiest port in the world. Many people call the country *Holland*. Yet Holland is the name of only two provinces, North Holland and South Holland.

The Dutch people of the Netherlands have built thousands of walls made of earth to keep the stormy North Sea from flooding their land. These walls are called *dikes*. A long arm of the North Sea, called the *Zuider Zee*, once extended into part of the Netherlands. Engineers turned it

▲ *Gouda, a traditional Dutch cheese, is taken in this old fashioned carrier during a cheese festival in the Netherlands.*

NETHERLANDS

Capital City: Amsterdam (694,000 people).
Area: 15,770 square miles (40,841 sq. km).
Population: 14,906,000.
Government: Monarchy.
Natural Resources: Oil and natural gas.
Export Products: Agricultural products, processed food, tobacco, natural gas, chemicals, metal products, clothing.
Unit of Money: Guilder (Florin).
Official Language: Dutch.

NETHERLANDS

into a freshwater lake, the *Ijsselmeer*, by building a 20-mile (32-km) dam to shut it off from the sea. Inside this lake and in other parts of the Netherlands are *polders*, lowlands formed when water was pumped out.

Windmills once pumped water out of the fields, but now electric pumps are mainly used. Canals beside the dikes carry off the water. Barges and sightseeing boats travel on the canals and rivers and some families live on the barges. The Dutch people enjoy ice skating on the frozen canals.

The Netherlands is one of the world's most crowded countries. Yet most people live well. Only in a few villages do people still wear the traditional baggy pants and wooden shoes, useful for working in wet fields.

The Netherlands is known for its delicious cheese and beautiful flowers. In spring, fields of blooming tulips and daffodils are a colorful sight. Flower bulbs are shipped all over the world. In addition to fishing, important industries are shipbuilding, machinery, textiles, electronics, chemicals, and oil refining. The Netherlands has a large merchant marine fleet. Amsterdam, the capital city, is a center for banking, business, and the diamond-cutting trade.

Since the sea is so much a part of their lives, the Dutch have been good seafarers and traders. In the 1600's, the Netherlands was a great sea power.

The Netherlands was ruled by Spain in the 1500's. The Dutch wanted their freedom and fought against Spain. In 1581, the northern part of the country declared itself independent. Spain finally recognized the country's independence in 1648.

The Netherlands is a constitutional monarchy. Queen Beatrix, who succeeded her mother, Queen Juliana, in 1980, is the present ruler. The queen shares the government with her council of ministers and a parliament. The center of government is at The Hague.

During World War II, the country suffered under German bombing. Working hard, the Dutch built a new, more prosperous nation after the war. The Dutch empire was effectively ended when Indonesia became independent in 1949, though the country still includes the self-governing Netherlands Antilles, two groups of Caribbean islands.

ALSO READ: AMSTERDAM, DAM, NORTH SEA, RHINE RIVER.

▶ *"God created the world, but the Dutch created Holland,"* is a saying in the Netherlands. The Dutch have reclaimed two-fifths of their country from the sea by building dikes around areas of shallow water and pumping the water into canals that flow into the sea beyond the dikes. These drained areas, or polders, *have become rich farmland.*